Assessing and Certifying Occupational Skills and Competences in Vocational Education and Training

ORGANISATION FOR ECONOMIC CO-OPERATION AND DEVELOPMENT

ORGANISATION FOR ECONOMIC CO-OPERATION AND DEVELOPMENT

Pursuant to Article 1 of the Convention signed in Paris on 14th December 1960, and which came into force on 30th September 1961, the Organisation for Economic Co-operation and Development (OECD) shall promote policies designed:

- to achieve the highest sustainable economic growth and employment and a rising standard of living in Member countries, while maintaining financial stability, and thus to contribute to the development of the world economy;
- to contribute to sound economic expansion in Member as well as non-member countries in the process of economic development; and
- to contribute to the expansion of world trade on a multilateral, non-discriminatory basis in accordance with international obligations.

The original Member countries of the OECD are Austria, Belgium, Canada, Denmark, France, Germany, Greece, Iceland, Ireland, Italy, Luxembourg, the Netherlands, Norway, Portugal, Spain, Sweden, Switzerland, Turkey, the United Kingdom and the United States. The following countries became Members subsequently through accession at the dates indicated hereafter: Japan (28th April 1964), Finland (28th January 1969), Australia (7th June 1971), New Zealand (29th May 1973), Mexico (18th May 1994) and the Czech Republic (21st December 1995). The Commission of the European Communities takes part in the work of the OECD (Article 13 of the OECD Convention).

Publié en français sous le titre :
QUALIFICATIONS ET COMPÉTENCES PROFESSIONNELLES DANS L'ENSEIGNEMENT TECHNIQUE ET LA FORMATION PROFESSIONNELLE
Évaluation et certification

FOREWORD

In 1990, the OECD launched a programme on the changing role of vocational and technical education and training (VOTEC). The activity included: country reports examining recent developments in national VOTEC systems and their responsiveness to changing jobs and needs of young people;[1] a cross-national study of educational pathways and participation in VOTEC; a study on the integration of practical and theoretical learning; and a series of international meetings providing lively information exchange and debates and culminating in a high-level conference in November 1994: "Vocational and Technical Education and Training for the 21st Century – Opening Pathways and Strengthening Professionalism".

Four policy seminars focused on the following themes of particular interest to OECD countries:

- linkages between various types and levels of general and vocational education and training;[2]
- implications of technological innovation for VOTEC;
- assessment, certification and recognition of skills and qualifications in VOTEC (this volume); and
- advantages and pitfalls of modern forms of apprenticeship.[3]

This volume contains a summary of work done under the third of these topics, the subject of a seminar jointly organised by Portugal's Education Ministry and the OECD in Porto in October 1992. Participants included representatives of relevant government departments and of employers and unions, as well as researchers.

The publication was prepared by Mr. Olivier Bertrand (consultant for the Centre d'études et de recherches sur les qualifications, CEREQ) under the direction of Mme Marianne Durand-Drouhin of the OECD. It is published on the responsibility of the Secretary-General of the OECD.

---

1. *Vocational Education and Training in the Netherlands: Reform and Innovation* and *Vocational Education in Germany: Modernisation and Responsiveness*, OECD, Paris, 1994.

TABLE OF CONTENTS

INTRODUCTION

The growing importance which many countries today attach to assessing training can be related to several recent trends. First, substantially expanding trainee numbers over recent decades have naturally put up the overall cost of training to the community. Understandably enough, then, the community has grown more concerned to assess the outcomes of what it invests in training and, in particular, to satisfy itself that training really is of the quality that industry and society expect.

At the same time, many countries are devolving responsibilities for training to regional and local authorities, and conferring a greater measure of autonomy on the training institutions themselves. If a country is to keep the various components of a training system in the right proportions, properly meshed in with one another and properly targeted on that country's needs, it is bound to require better assessments of what the training system is actually achieving, and that is one of the functions that certification should perform.

As information technologies spread, as competition intensifies and as the ways in which work is organised evolve, employers are asking for a radically different mix of skills. They are increasingly concerned that skills be tailored to their requirements and are looking to certification for appropriate information about the skills trainees have actually acquired.

In addition, young people's expectations of training have evolved and diversified, while adult training is moving increasingly to the fore. Economic globalisation, and the movement of information and of workers, are making skill recognition and transferability still more urgent an issue.

All this has had the effect of generating new and somewhat conflicting demands on certification systems: they are having to deal with a larger and more varied population, and must reconcile their concern not to marginalise parts of that population with their concern to guarantee that training really is of the required standard. The system is supposed, at the same time, to remain simple, easily workable and not too expensive.

It was against this background that the Porto seminar participants were invited to look particularly at four topics, described in preparatory papers:

- pedagogical aspects of certification: examinations and testing procedures;
- recognition of qualifications in the labour market;
- transferability of qualifications to alternative employment opportunities;
- the institutional problems that assessment and certification can pose.

In discussion, the first point to emerge was that problems of communication could arise, especially over the meanings of expressions like qualification or skill.

These are actually not so much problems of terminology or language as conceptual problems; even within Member countries, many of the concepts are hazy. Clarifying conceptual problems is hence a prerequisite for any kind of comparative analysis.

That is especially so because, as at other OECD VOTEC (Vocational and Technical Education and Training) programme meetings, the discussion revealed that circumstances in Member countries, and in particular their training systems, varied quite considerably. The form which certification arrangements actually take is bound to mirror the overall design of a country's training system and the aims assigned to it. Depending on the country under consideration, and on how vocational training fits into the system as a whole, the function of certification may be largely to ensure that qualifications are recognised for employment purposes (that is, recognised by the labour market and more particularly by industry), or it may be to accredit a given level or a given occupational skill.

Similarly, industry's role in designing and implementing certification can vary a great deal from one country to another, reflecting whatever role that country's industry plays in shaping and supplying training. Clearly, too, certification cannot take the same form under a federal system of government, where training will not necessarily be the same across the whole country, as under a central system.

In other words, no one method is ideal and countries must take account of their own particular backgrounds in adjusting their certification systems. Having said that, though, the point is well worth making that, just as in other fields on which VOTEC work impinges, most OECD Member countries are proceeding in a number of common directions. One notable instance is a concern to make training systems more flexible, prompting several countries to introduce certification systems that are more modular. Other instances are a feeling that vocational training should be based on broader foundations and, as already noted, the trends towards greater decentralisation of responsibility for training and more adult training.

Countries which are developing adult training become increasingly aware that adults and young people have different needs. The broader competence of adults is also recognised, not only whatever training they may have undergone but also their experience. Research in the United Kingdom and other English-speaking countries to develop forms of assessment in terms of what people can actually do thus becomes especially relevant, as does American countries' experience of recognising immigrant workers' qualifications.

A further point is that all OECD countries are having to address the problem of how general education should relate to vocational training and, within that, the particular issue of how the young see general education and vocational training. This latter has been a recurring theme in other VOTEC-related meetings.

The certification system as such raises issues of defining responsibilities and choosing procedures. On the responsibilities side, the main problem is what role industry should be playing in training and certification. Most countries are seeking to meet industry's needs by tailoring their training courses and having a certification system that can provide clear, reliable information. Involving employers or their representatives in mapping out what directions training should be moving along, or at least involving them in the examination process, is becoming an increasingly plain necessity.

But putting that principle into practice does generate certain problems. It depends on how industrial relations stand, and in particular raises the issue of smaller businesses, which cannot usually offer the full gamut of training and assessment possibilities. Another problem can arise from the potential conflict between the certification system's need to be broadly understandable, and therefore fairly consistent over time, and its need to be responsive to changing labour market requirements. A further issue is how certification should relate to pay levels.

Looking at certification options raises a series of questions: should training establishments be responsible for assessing their trainees internally, or should that be a function for some outside body which could be expected to assess them more objectively? Should assessment be a once-for-all process or should trainees be continuously assessed? Should examinations be written or oral, and how far can the two be combined? Should trainees be assessed on what they know, on what they can do, or on what skills they possess? How can practical skills be assessed?*

Looking beyond national borders, the question of recognition also arises for students and workers who have qualified abroad. This is of especial concern to those countries participating in the building of European unity.

This volume is in two parts. Part I contains some general, across-the-board analytical material, and Part II presents relevant illustrations from a range of OECD countries.

Part I includes the preparatory studies and contributions, mainly on the broader issues, together with the reports from the four working groups. Hilary Steedman's introductory paper sets the broad scene and outlines questions for the seminar to address. This is supplemented by papers on four special aspects:

- Gabriel Fragnière discusses some awkward problems of definition arising out of the concepts of qualification, skill, assessment and certification.

- Problems of implementing a certification system are described by Sheila Clarke and Ron Tuck, representing Scotland.

- Olivier Bertrand reports on how the comparability and recognition of qualifications are being addressed at the European level.

---

* These points are also discussed in *Apprenticeship: Which Way Forward?*, OECD, Paris, 1994.

– Luis Imaginario's contribution mainly reviews the differences in understanding and interpreting the concept of certification, both in Portugal and from the standpoint of European integration.

Part I is supplemented by reports from the working groups focusing more closely on each of the four seminar topics. Part II contains the main reports from participating countries. The aim here was not to give another account of national training systems but to provide a basis for substantive discussion. Presentations selected are those which best illustrate the analyses in Part I in different national contexts.

What these and other VOTEC-related activities suggest is that there are broadly three patterns, or perhaps three institutional and cultural approaches to vocational training: a pattern based on Germany's dual system, another English-speaking pattern which is less institutionalised and more decentralised; and a third pattern based mainly on the school system in a number of Latin and Scandinavian countries.

The dual-system pattern is illustrated here by two papers which together give a very full picture of how it operates in assessing, accrediting and recognising qualifications. Germany's presentation provides a detailed description of the institutional background and of how the system actually works in practice. Austria's contribution presents a slightly different system, highlighting some of the deeper issues arising out of the Austrian presentation to the seminar.

The approach in English-speaking countries is illustrated by two very different papers. The United States contribution outlines the problems involved in the gradual and voluntary introduction of a nationwide system of certification in a federal country having no such system but in which the need for one is starting to be felt. The New Zealand contribution gives a description of a national system of qualifications based on vocational skills, patterned on the United Kingdom model. New Zealand's new system was just being introduced at the time of the seminar.

The third approach is illustrated in a presentation by the French Ministry of Education. This analyses the pros and cons of a centralised certification system for essentially school-based training and describes current attempts to improve the system, especially by taking account of skills acquired outside school.

The skills recognition issue, with which the seminar was especially concerned, is covered in greater detail by two of the country papers reproduced in Part II. From the Netherlands contribution we have included extracts showing how the Netherlands is addressing skills recognition for adults. The contribution from Canada (Quebec) looks more closely at recognition for an immigration country receiving students and workers who had done their initial training abroad.

Part I

A. THE ISSUES AND A SYNTHESIS
OF THE DISCUSSIONS

THE ISSUES

by

Hilary Steedman
National Institute of Economic and Social Research, London

INTRODUCTION

Section One of this paper provides a framework for the discussion of problems of assessment, certification and recognition of occupational skills and competences. Section Two attempts the task of conceptual clarification of the key issues. The third section looks at issues raised by the changing needs of employers and incentives that encourage individuals to invest in skills. The final section explores the four themes of the seminar and poses the key questions for discussion.

1. THE FRAMEWORK OF ANALYSIS

A discussion of issues of assessment, certification and recognition of occupational competences should not lose sight of the profound changes in all industrialised countries which have led to these issues becoming a focus of national debate in almost all the countries represented here. It is worthwhile to briefly restate the main elements.

In the course of the last 25 years, the electronically controlled automation of industrial processes and of business information have made possible the production of a wider variety of higher-quality goods at prices lower than was possible in the past. At the same time, and as a result of the same technological factors, living standards have risen, and demand or higher quality and greater variety has increased to a new level.

Firms and businesses have attempted – more or less successfully – to transform their traditional modes of production. At the level of the individual employee, a production worker no longer carries out a few clearly defined and largely unchanging tasks but must now perform a whole series of operations, not all of which can be defined in advance. In the various market sectors, global leaders are those who – unless they enjoy some notable comparative advantage – have most successfully developed the skills of the whole work force to take full advantage of the potential of new technology. Those competing in the same markets have been obliged to try to follow the same path with degrees of success dependent to a large extent not only on their own efforts but on the suitability of the training infrastructure in their country.

Policy makers must take into consideration these fundamental changes. First, the existing skills and competences of a substantial part of the current work force are inappropriate to meet these new skill requirements. Second, this substantial section of the work force has, on the whole, received a low level of general education in the compulsory school system and little or no subsequent training. The costs of attempting to upgrade their skills are correspondingly heavy, and the role of assessment and certification in relation to mature emplojyees poses special problems which will be spelt out in more detail below.

To what extent are firms able to meet and overcome this challenge without the intervention of the State and support from public funds? The evidence here is not encouraging. The identification of the "low-skills, low-quality" equilibrium (Finegold, D. and Soskice, D. [1988], "The failure of training in Britain: analysis and prescription", *Oxford Review of Economic Policy,* Vol. 4, Autumn, pp. 21-53) shows how firms become locked into the sort of standardised production for mass markets that a low level of work force skill encourages and how, without changes in the training infrastructure at national level, movement to a "high-skills, high-quality" equilibrium is unlikely to occur. The arguments about externalities are well enough known for it not to be necessary to rehearse them here. The facts are that the failure of firms and individuals in many industrialised countries to make decisions about investment in training, which would rectify this imbalance, underlines the difficulty of exclusive reliance on market forces to regulate the supply of skills.

Many industrialised countries face a situation where, in a number of industrial and commercial sectors, firms need to move rapidly from the low-skills/low-quality equilibrium appropriate to the era of mechanisation to a new equilibrium appropriate to the era of flexible specialisation. In this process of transition, analysis of recent experience of advanced industrialised countries indicates that institutions play a key role in creating the conditions which will encourage firms and individuals to invest in training for skills. These institutional arrangements will frequently (but not exclusively) be the results of action by publicly elected or appointed authorities at local, regional or national level – or sometimes all three. Public policy which "oils the wheels" or substitutes for private training is usually concerned with three aspects of occupational skills: legislation and financial instruments, provision of training facilities and personnel, and assessment and certification. This paper assumes a leading – but not necessarily predominant – role for the State in maintaining assessment and certification. The extent to which government should seek to maintain a monopoly position in this field is raised later in the paper.

Until now in this paper, the needs of individuals as members of society with legitimate expectations of opportunity for self-development and career progression have not been addressed. These issues are of primary importance to all members of society, whether finding a first job, being employed or seeking a job as a result of unemployment. Making such opportunities fully available will also serve the best interests of the economy.

The extent to which any society can meet the expectations of personal and career development of young people and adults is not independent of how well that same society enables its work force to adapt to technological changes. Countries which adapt rapidly and successfully to the demands of new technology are not only able to offer their members higher living standards but they have more resources from which to finance further development and upgrading of skills. Those countries suffering to any degree from a "low-skills/low-quality" equilibrium will initially have fewer resources to devote to enabling individuals to develop their skills and improve their career prospects. For countries closed to any extent in this vicious circle of skills and quality, the requirement of cost-effective management of training provision will act as a major constraint upon the extent to which certification and assessment of occupational competence can cater for a wide variety of individual needs.

The task of this publication is to advance our understanding of how assessment and certification can contribute to moving as far as possible towards the two objectives of economic growth and personal career development. In our discussions, we hoped to learn how researchers, advisers and those concerned with implementing policy in this area in different countries have worked to remove or minimise constraints on progress towards these objectives. In understanding how this has been achieved, we can gain insight into the necessary weighing-up of costs and benefits involved. By applying these insights to our own situation as appropriate, we can learn positive lessons from the experiences of others and short-circuit the process of trial and error in policy-making and implementation that is often costly and damaging.

The policy objectives explored above constitute the wider framework of common aims which are most appropriate for promoting positive debate.

To summarise, these objectives are:

- to rapidly transform the skills of the existing work force and to prepare all participants to cope with rapid future change in the demand for skills;
- to make provision for individuals to develop to the full their potential for contributing to society through participation in paid employment;
- to develop and implement high-quality education and training provision to achieve these objectives in a way which makes the best use of scarce resources.

2. THE CHALLENGE TO THOSE ENGAGED IN EDUCATION AND TRAINING – RESOURCES, CURRICULUM AND PEDAGOGY

The increasing demand from young people for training

Educators, young people and all those involved in planning and providing for them have been confronted with problems of continuous expansion for at least ten to fifteen years in many if not all OECD countries. The young people now staying on in full-time education and/or training have very different aptitudes and attainments from those of twenty years ago.

The very different attainments of the "new" entrants to post-secondary education require colleges to offer a much broader range of courses than previously. The need is to challenge all students without placing upon them demands which they will be unable to meet. This need has been met in many countries with skilful planning of programmes.

Despite the best efforts of providers and teachers, some students may still be excluded because the courses offered do not attract them, because they do not have the financial resources to continue or because their prior school attainments are inadequate. It is necessary to consider ways of bringing these young people into education and training, and the great variety of experience that can be brought to this problem from OECD countries is of great value in this discussion.

Teachers and other educators are continually seeking new ways of helping their students to learn. The challenge of new client groups has brought out many valuable experiments in teaching. Some countries have experimented with short modular units and student choice, while others have experimented with computer-aided learning. Others again have intensified their efforts to help young people to learn while retaining a tried and trusted pedagogical method. An objective look must be taken at what changes are really effective in helping students.

Young people are of particular concern because their needs in relation to assessment and certification differ in some quite fundamental respects from the needs of adults. A rapidly growing trend in all industrialised countries is the tendency for young people to voluntarily remain in full- or part-time education or in education and training after the end of compulsory schooling. This trend throws into sharp relief the anomaly (surviving from a previous stage of development of educational provision) of prescribing completely different pathways with no common elements for those following work-related training or vocational programmes and those following programmes of "academic" education designed to qualify them to proceed to similar programmes at a higher level. Assessment and certification should be planned with progression and switching (from one occupation to another and from "academic" to work-related and *vice versa*) very much in mind. However, the new circumstances of (in many countries) more than half of all 16 to 18 year-olds still in formal education or education and training underlines the need for certification of work-related education and training for young people to be designed in such a way that:

   a) all young people receive general education in key areas such as mathematics, their own and a foreign language to a fairly similar level so as to encourage flexibility and the ability to adapt to as yet unknown work developments;

   b) all young people are offered opportunities for "switching" as defined above, b) being very much dependent on a) being already in place.

Various models do exist in OECD countries of ways of trying to achieve these objectives. Again, certain constraints operate which it may be helpful to try to spell out.

Often with the purpose of improving the status of work-related programmes, the general academic requirements of those programmes are pitched at a level of difficulty which is higher than that required to meet the objective of future flexibility and adaptability outlined above and which thereby excludes a significant proportion of young people from following such programmes successfully. This in turn raises the question, much debated in the United Kingdom for example, of whether certification of vocational education and training should be assimilated to the certification already well established for "academic" programmes, or whether vocational certification should be based on completely different criteria. If the first option is chosen, a) and b) above are easier to achieve, but a problem of exclusion of those with low academic attainments arises.

If the second option is chosen, experience shows that a more "inclusive" (in the sense of practically the whole age group being able to obtain certification) system results, but a) and b) are difficult to implement.

One way of trying to achieve adaptability and "switching" is to award certification on the basis of modules of learning, some of which can be common to those following either type of programme. Modules represent in some ways an attractive solution to some of the problems outlined above, but again there are costs which need to be spelt out.

Modules allow students (both young people and adults) to carry forward parts of a programme which they may have successfully completed and to complete the full certificate at a later point when, for example, funds or time are forthcoming. An argument is also put forward that assessment at the end of a short module represents a fairer method of assessment than a year-end examination. Modules can also be more easily assessed by continuous assessment based on classwork or by assessment based on coursework – modes of assessment which many support as offering a more valid assessment than a single written examination. The content or syllabus of modules can, of course, be just as tightly prescribed and assessment can be carried out as reliably as for single unified programmes of study. Combinations of modules can also be prescribed, and reliability of assessment and certification need not differ from that of more traditional modes. Higher costs and reduced teaching time associated with modular assessment must, of course, be borne in mind.

More problematic is the "pick 'n mix" approach to vocational certification also made possible by a modular structure. For assessment and certification, this approach raises problems of information loss, since the variability of content of a modular certificate may confuse those wishing to make inferences about vocational skills and knowledge. An even more fragmented assessment results from an "individualised learning" approach often used to adapt formal education and training provision to very variable levels of student attainment on entry. The possible gain in achievement of some (probably a minority of students) must be weighed against the administrative complexity and forward planning difficulties inherent in allowing students very wide choice, and the difficulty of achieving recognition of the certificate awarded.

Changing demands of society

Employers increasingly look to the education system to provide the higher levels of skill and education that they require. This trend places the educational institutions, their practices and their standards under the public spotlight. They are increasingly scrutinised for the reliability of their certification procedures and the validity of the certification awarded. They may be pressed to introduce new forms of assessment, e.g. continuous assessment which places great demands on staff and poses serious problems for standards and reliability.

Another pressure on colleges and educators are considerations of cost and the requirement to work within tight budgets. Colleges have traditionally put the needs of their students first; however, the requirement to meet costs from revenue generated may lead them to lower their standards in order to meet output targets of certificates. We need to discuss ways of safeguarding standards in an increasingly harsh economic climate for educational institutions.

As the demand for certification grows on employers' needs for skills, so employers increasingly expect that certification will mean up-to-date industrial and commercial competences. Institutions inevitably experience difficulties in responding rapidly to change, since they represent stability. Much benefit is derived from qualified and experienced personnel, and this requirement sits uneasily with the demand for education and training to match rapidly changing needs. Educators, providers and planners face a difficult task in trying to be responsive without undermining their own institutions.

These changes have given rise to a widespread appreciation of the need for two-way communication between employers and institutions. This is not easy to achieve, given the constraints on time of all involved and the very different backgrounds from which educators and employers are often drawn. Many different ways of bringing together employers and educators have been thought out and put into practice in Member countries, and these need to be explored and evaluated in discussion.

An increasing demand from adult employees and from those seeking employment
employment

In many OECD countries, full-time post-secondary institutions of training and education have been reserved almost exclusively for young people (not in all countries, however – in the United Kingdom and Denmark for example, post-16 colleges enrol young people and adults). In some countries, colleges will need to find ways of responding to the need for upgrading adult skills.

Where adult employees are concerned, the need is overwhelmingly for short, focused, specialist training which is highly responsive to the needs of businesses. Often, employees cannot be spared from the job, and training must be provided in the work place or at unorthodox times, for example weekends. In some countries, special structures have been set up to enable colleges to respond to these needs. Nevertheless, logistical and administrative problems are formidable and much could be learnt from countries with experience in this field. Some of these issues are dealt with later in the paper.

However, with colleges wishing to award to all their students a recognised and valid certificate and to assess this reliably, if training takes place in the work place, or courses are "tailor-made" for particular employers, then this causes difficulties for valid certification. The solutions that planners and providers have found to these problems will need to be explained and evaluated.

3.   ASSESSMENT AND CERTIFICATION OF OCCUPATIONAL SKILLS

Issues raised by the needs of employers

We can summarise the situation in many industrialised countries as follows: On the supply side there is an active labour force more or less adapted to new demands, and successive cohorts of young entrants to adult life more or less prepared to meet the new flexible requirements for skills. On the demand side are the firms themselves, whose short-term interests in remaining at existing skill levels are probably in conflict with their long-term interest in moving to a high-quality equilibrium. Experience shows that, without public intervention, neither individuals nor firms are likely to be able to take the measures needed to move to a new "high-skills/high-quality" equilibrium. Public intervention cannot be random and spontaneous; it must operate on the basis of a defined strategy systematically implemented and open to public scrutiny. The interaction of public institutions and private or firm behaviour determines the success or failure of efforts to improve economic growth through skill development.

It is at this interface, between the behaviour and decisions of individuals, firms, private and public bodies and institutions, that assessment and certification operate in the training for skills. Here, certification at its most effective performs a number of tasks. First, it enables the two key groups in the labour market to communicate effectively. A primary purpose of a certificate of skills is to convey information between those seeking to buy and sell skills – employees and employers. With millions of transactions taking place every year, the first requirement of such a system is simplicity, clarity and consistency over time. Employers – the people who sell and buy skills – do not usually have the time to learn the niceties of a complex and ever-changing system of skill certification.

Simplicity, clarity and consistency over time are necessary but not sufficient conditions for a certificate to successfully facilitate bringing together employees with skills and employers seeking skills. Unless the employer considers the certificate worthy of recognition, he/she will not be willing to rely upon it for decisions about employment or wage levels. The certificate will not do its job of conveying information to individuals in the labour market about the value employers place on skills unless the employer distinguishes the holders of certain certificates by employing them in preference to those with no certificate and by paying them more.

For the certificate to successfully and efficiently convey information in a two-way process between firms and potential employees, firms must recognise the skills it certifies as relevant and the assessment as valid and reliable. It is convenient for this analysis to summarise these qualities as recognition and to take as axiomatic to our discussions that vocational certification is worthless without recognition in the sense defined here.

Issues of validity and reliability

The requirement that assessment and certification of vocational skills achieve employer recognition of relevance constitutes one of the major constraints that policy makers concerned with the institutional infrastructure of vocational education and training must consider. A simple form of certification can convey only a limited amount of information. Yet the employer needs to know whether a potential recruit can really do the job in hand. The amount of information he/she would ideally like to have is very great – the amount that he/she realistically has time to absorb is small. Can all the information employers would ideally like to have ever be conveyed by certification? If the certificate seeks to convey a great deal of information about skills, can its reliability be guaranteed? Should certification sacrifice reliability for validity? Is it possible to assess ability to do a job in such a way that an employer can place complete confidence in such an assessment? Are the costs involved in attempting to produce a valid assessment justified? These are some of the questions raised by equating the need to convey complex information with that of presenting it in an easily recognisable form in which the employer can have confidence.

Issues of reliability and validity have always preoccupied those concerned with the theory and practice of assessment. But the problem of validity is more acute in the case of the certification of skills, since what is to be certified is a completely different type of activity from that tested by writing an examination paper. But formal assessment and certification in industrialised societies originated with educational institutions, working to narrow definitions of competence usually characterised as "academic", *i.e.* capacity for abstract reasoning conveyed through written or spoken language. Reliable means of assessment of academic skills – the common written paper – were not difficult to develop. Since these assessments were originally intended primarily to certify permission to pass from one level of the education system to the next, they were appropriate for that purpose. But the skills required of an employee in industry or commerce are far more diverse than the narrow requirements of the formal education system.

Can traditional forms of assessment by written examination (admittedly with high degrees of reliability) provide sufficient proof of the skills that employers seek in their employees? One test of this proposition would be to identify countries where a high degree of employer recognition of vocational certificates is found together with certification based principally on assessment by written examination. In this case, the certificate itself seeks to communicate directly only a small amount of information about the potential employee. However, we know that where certification is based on written assessment, employers infer from the certificate a great deal more than is actually stated. Since this inference is based on past experience of employees with similar certificates, the extent to which they will feel able to make such inferences will depend on how recently and frequently title and/or content of certification has been changed, and on how much confidence employers have in the reliability and consistency of standards over time (and often over geographical areas).

Issues raised by changing skill needs

With certificates which "display" vocational skills, it would be most advantageous from the point of view of information about individuals if the examination syllabus changed as little as possible over time. Yet, we have already made clear that certification must correspond to employers' current needs and that these requirements are likely to be changing rapidly as a result of new technology. A simple form of assessment and certification by proxy may not cope well with the need for change and relevance.

A more complex form of assessment and certification which does not require the employer to make inferences on the basis of the certificate, but spells out in full each and every competence certified, offers substantial advantages in this respect. The list of competences can simply be updated as requirements change, and employers will continue to understand from the certificate what they are "buying". Some disadvantages of this approach are cost and complexity of assessment procedures, and loss of reliability and consistency of certification over time. These issues would merit further exploration.

Incentives to individuals to invest in skills

Certification should convey good-quality, reliable and relevant information about what individuals are likely to be able to do in the work place. At the same time, it should be simple and "transparent", so that individuals can make rational decisions about investment in acquiring certification. It should also offer individuals a variety of occupational objectives of sufficient degrees of difficulty or complexity to ensure that whatever his/her initial attainments, a realistic, achievable and worthwhile target is widely available to all who wish to invest their time and energy. To offer the maximum incentive to individuals to invest, provision also needs to be made for career progression leading to higher levels of responsibility and wages and also for a possible change of track or occupation.

These constraints imply that certification needs to be established at a number of levels within a coherent overall framework and that the requirements at one level form the foundation or starting point for the next level up. A market in certification with competing examination bodies often produces the very reverse of a coherent and transparent system. In many countries, one publicly responsible authority has responsibility for establishing such a framework. The requirement of coherence and transparency, which is at least as important as the necessity to ensure that certificated skills correspond to employers' needs, adds considerably to the complexity of arranging for a successful system of certification.

If the system is also required to respond in a highly flexible manner to local needs and the requirements of new work organisation, then the complexity of frequently revising and upgrading a whole interlocking system of qualifications may prove unmanageable. In addition, too rapid and too complex a change overloads certification as an information system and leads to breakdown. It will certainly be possible to find, among OECD Members, examples both of excessively stable hierarchical systems of vocational qualification and of extremely unstable systems where the relations between each element are uncertain. Debate needs to focus on the extent to which change can be accommodated within a coherent and transparent system.

It is of course widely recognised that formal programmes of training allow us to "short-circuit", on the basis of accumulated and systematised experience, the much longer process of acquiring skills by observation and by trial and error on the job. While we may hope to offer systematic training to most young people entering the labour market, the vast majority of the work force in many OECD countries have received no formal training either on or off the job. It would naturally be wrong to assume that employees have therefore acquired no occupational skills. Many have gained considerable expertise and may legitimately expect to be accorded the formal recognition of certification for those skills. In addition, employers may wish to make available training to add on new skills.

The assessment and certification of the skills of experienced employees raises different issues from those associated with young people. For a start, it is not clear that the same demands of a general education should be made of adults whose skills acquired on the job are to be recognised by certification. This means that the certification designed for young people may not be suitable for adult employees without modification. Yet, in the interests of clarity and consistency, it is desirable to simplify vocational certification as far as possible. Ways in which adult employees can be brought within a single system of certification without unreasonable assessments being imposed constitute another important area for debate.

The upgrading of skills is usually financed by employers and it is well known that in these cases, employers are often reluctant to offer nationally recognised certification for fear of losing scarce skills to other firms which are prepared to bid for their employees by offering higher wages ("poaching"). If some contribution is made to employers' training costs out of public funds, it is feasible to require employers to offer in return a nationally recognised certificate. If this is not the case, then intervention is difficult and probably undesirable (stringent requirements for certificates might discourage employers from offering any training to employees). The experience of some OECD countries shows that there is a role for public intervention by loans and subsidies to encourage such initiatives.

Encouraging employees to invest in skill upgrading

If a system is in place which offers recognised additional certification to established employees for which they can acquire the necessary skills and knowledge in their own time, then the problem of non-certification of additional skills acquired by employees is overcome to a quite considerable extent. For this policy to be successful, not only must the provision of certification be appropriate, but pay differentials and career opportunities within firms must provide suitable incentives.

We have seen that recognition of vocational qualifications by employers is effectively signalled by their willingness to pay more for certificated skills. In some countries, recognition has been institutionalised in collective agreements which bind employers to offer certain differentials in acknowledgment of certificates obtained. It is notable that, in those countries, there is less difficulty in persuading individuals to invest in training, both in initial training and in training for additional occupational skills, and that the supply of individuals with occupational skill certificates is thereby increased.

Such rigidities undoubtedly have disadvantages. It is often difficult – and sometimes impossible – for adults who have failed to obtain a vocational certificate at the usual age to compensate by obtaining it at a later date. Mobility on the external labour market may thus be restricted. In addition, recognition in collective agreements gives rise to added complexity of negotiations between employer and employee organisations when any major change in systems of assessment and certification is required. However, if access to the qualifications in question can be made freely available to all comers, by a sufficiently flexible system of assessment and certification, then it may be felt that the advantages on balance outweigh the disadvantages. A further issue is thus whether a country wishing to achieve a rapid rate of growth of individuals with occupational skills should seriously consider encouraging employer and employee organisations to reach such agreements.

Defining occupational skills: ends and means

Certificates should attest to relevant skills if employers are to recognise them. A single, usually publicly controlled body is an efficient way of ensuring a simple, stable and reliable system of certification. However, because, by its nature, a public body attempts to provide for the whole of a national or regional territory, and because of the inertia built in to other associated arrangements of teaching and assessing, such bodies may find it hard to determine relevant occupational skills and equally hard to adjust assessment and certification rapidly enough. Furthermore, public bodies may effectively be in the position of a monopoly provider of certification, so that employers' dissatisfaction with the content of certification cannot be adequately signalled by switching to another provider.

In some systems, and particularly in those where occupational skill certificates are acquired largely through full-time college-based courses, public authorities appear to have tacitly recognised this dilemma and to have decided that the costs of continually updating outweigh the benefits. They have instead concentrated on providing transferable general skills at the expense of work place specific training. This allows the certificate to compensate for lack of relevance by increased reliability and transparency. In addition, where assessment is based on skills and knowledge acquired in college, quality assurance and the maintenance of standards over time is easier to manage. Where some or all assessment and certification is based on learning which takes place on the job, relevance is easier to achieve but there is inevitably some loss of reliability, and quality assurance is more difficult and costly. A major issue is the search for a realistic balance between relevant work place skills on the one hand, and reliability and adequate quality assurance of assessment and certification on the other.

Where certification takes place on the basis of full-time college attendance, the training providers work at some remove from those engaged in industrial or commercial production and services. The skills of the trainers may become outdated and course content may no longer be relevant. At the same time, there is a need to encourage employers to reflect on occupational skill requirements in the longer term and to articulate these in a way which makes communication with providers and those in charge of assessment and certification as effective as possible. The contribution of employee organisations to this process as a way of conveying the perspective of the individual in the work place is also important, and ways of bringing providers of certification, employer representatives and employee representatives together should be explored. Almost all advanced industrialised countries have recognised these problems and devised ways of attempting to avoid or remedy these weaknesses in the chain linking skills and certification.

The tension inherent in systems of certification which aim both for stability and reliability and for response to local labour market needs is also an important issue. It was emphasized above that the individual employee requires a widely recognised certificate which will enable him/her to move within a single firm and from one employer to another.

It has been noted that training provided by employers to employees may consist largely of firm-specific skills and may not lead to certification. However, in some cases, employers might wish to offer certification but are unable to find the appropriate means. Such certification could well assist workers to be more mobile, since not all employers are anxious to hold their employees at all costs. Should systems of certification be adapted to take account of this problem by trying to accommodate even the simplest and most job-specific of occupational skills?

Certificates which recognise single skills or separate-skill elements may well be highly suitable for acknowledging the skills adults have acquired on the job and thereby promoting mobility. Such skills are likely to be of only limited relevance to future requirements for flexibility and adaptability. Excessive emphasis on the skills of the existing work force as the starting point for defining occupational skills for the purpose of certification may lead to the institutionalisation of prevailing skill levels instead of progress towards new and more sophisticated work force skills. In addition to the effect on levels or standards of skill, the certification of single-skill elements for adult employees is difficult to reconcile with the requirements for the preparation of young people to enter work, outlined above. Yet any certificate of occupational skills should fit into a wider, progressive framework, and the system as a whole should aim for maximum simplicity. Should certification systems aim to accommodate the need of experienced employees for single-skill certification and, if so, how and where should it be situated within this overall framework?

The coming of the Single European Market has raised in more acute form a problem which has actually been largely unresolved since the signing of the Treaty of Rome – the need for a system of mutual recognition of qualifications which will facilitate the movement of workers within the European Union. Many factors complicate this search, not least of which is how much certification has become part of institutionalised labour market regulation in the EU member states and the very real differences in requirement for certification and mode of delivery in each country.

4. THE THEMES OF DISCUSSION

Theme I: Implications of different approaches to assessment and certification certification

The issues outlined above affect teachers, their institutions, the way they teach, and their relationship with their students at every level of the education and training system. In most countries, a well-established tradition of liberal education having as its aim the development of the individual and introduction to their own culture and society will already be in place. Whereas traditionally a certain distance was maintained between the demands of the labour market and the work of teachers in schools and colleges, the increased demand for employees with good general skills and greater flexibility means that the content of educational programmes for young people and their traditional modes of assessment – the written examination – are coming under greater scrutiny from employers, from parents concerned that school is not preparing students for today's labour market, and from governments preoccupied with national efficiency.

The written examination, externally set and marked, requiring candidates to demonstrate ability to convey understanding by means of well-constructed answers is still the dominant mode of assessment of mainstream "academic" schooling and has served the purpose of identifying those qualified to proceed to the next stage of education in a fairly satisfactory way. In addition, it is claimed that employers used school examination results to pick out potential employees with high general ability, without being concerned with the exact nature of the specific skills that might be certified by the examination (screening). However, schools and colleges are increasingly called upon to teach a variety of related and specific vocational competences and, from the start of this process, it has been recognised that the formal written examination cannot adequately assess such skills. A variety of responses to this problem have been developed in OECD countries.

Some responses insist on students passing a formal written test as well as an assessment of practical performance in a set piece of work by external assessors (e.g. Germany). Other countries also insist on the two components of assessment of vocational skill – the written knowledge test and the practical performance test – but allow partial certification of the practical element on the grounds that an individual may be adequately skilled in their own occupational area without being able to complete the written test (e.g. France). Whatever its value in conveying information about what the candidate can do (and many experts in assessment criticize all time-restricted written examinations because they reveal very little about what candidates can do outside the examination room), few countries dispense entirely with written tests for vocational certificates. Recently, however, an innovative new system of occupational competence assessment in the United Kingdom has been introduced which assesses candidates entirely on performance and requires no written test. The claim, which will be readily understood by those who have wrestled with these problems, is that this form of assessment is more valid, i.e. it tells the consumer what the person can do more effectively than a certificate based on an examination. The implications of this form of assessment for the organisation and implementation of assessment is the subject of Theme IV below.

The tendency for a majority of young people to stay on for general or vocational education beyond age 16 was mentioned earlier. Their expectations are increasingly of a system which offers both choice, opportunity for progression and parity of provision. Clearly, these objectives become more problematic once it has been accepted that practical tests of performance need to form a part of vocational assessment. In many countries, the authorities would like to offer all young people aged 18 to 19 the same certificate or a separate certification of equal status. With assessment of vocational competence dependent on tests of practical performance, the traditional "academic" assessment by examination begins to look very different from the newer performance-related criterion-based testing. The case for according equal status to the two types of qualification becomes more difficult to sustain. Different countries have sought and implemented various solutions to the problem of parity of esteem for vocational and academic post-secondary qualifications. At the one extreme – as suggested above – formal examinations are insisted upon for both vocational and general academic certification. At the other – as in the United Kingdom – the form which assessment takes diverges radically. Other countries have tried to blur the so-called dividing line between the academic and vocational, perhaps by introducing modular programmes where students can "pick 'n mix".

General academic programmes have been followed mainly by young people, and have been offered often only on a full-time basis requiring several years of continuous study. Programmes leading to vocational certificates need to be made available to a much wider public, including adults returning to work and with heavy domestic responsibilities, full-time mature employees and persons with very little prior formal education. This means that, if the same form of vocational certification is to be offered to all these different groups in addition to being offered to young people, assessment needs to be more flexible than that traditionally provided at the end of full-time secondary schooling. Again, small modular units may be the best vehicle for the teaching and learning of vocational competence and skills, and the classroom may not be the best location – the college workshop or the work place may provide the most appropriate teaching and learning environment.

In fact, the requirements of this very diverse clientele and the practical work-related subject matter may strongly imply that assessment should take place outside the school/college setting altogether and may also call into question whether full-time teachers with an academic training should undertake the examining and certification at all. In a number of countries, the assessment of vocational competence – whether of young people or of adults, takes place outside the educational setting altogether and is carried out – in the case of the United Kingdom – by the trainee's supervisor. The further that assessment moves from the educational setting, the more difficult it becomes to provide for transfer from one track to another or for progression based upon a number of units, some vocational and some academic. Again, OECD countries have all confronted this problem and explored different solutions. The working groups need to understand the implications of the different solutions for all the social groups concerned and to try to evaluate the optimal answer to the variety of needs and pressures involved.

The introduction of the assessment of occupational competence purely on the basis of performance in the work place raises the important question of whether a collection of competences "adds up" to what is understood as "skills". What do we understand a skilled individual to be able to do? Do we expect him/her to have at his/her disposal a body of theoretical knowledge underpinning skills and do we expect the skilled individual to be able to demonstrate that knowledge by expounding and explaining coherently to an audience either orally or in writing or both? Many would argue that the skilled craftsman can be a master of his/her trade without being able to construct a coherent sentence. On the other hand, others would maintain that, in a world of rapidly changing occupational demands, the ability to master a body of abstract knowledge and to communicate it to others is a vital skill in itself which all should be encouraged to acquire. The argument for requiring the individual seeking vocational certification to undergo formal examination in general subjects may rest more upon the view that such skills promote flexibility and are bound to be required in the future. The authorities in some OECD countries are obviously clearly of this view, whereas others are less convinced.

Questions debated by the working groups

- Can the traditional examination provide adequate information on students' suitability for employment – as opposed to mere "screening"?
- Should written examinations form part of the requirement for vocational certification?
- How can "parity of esteem" of different types of post-16 programmes be achieved?
- Must parity of esteem be based upon college-based assessment and certification or can it be based upon learning and testing in the work place?
- Should the same vocational certificate be available to young people in college or in training and to adult employees and returnees? If so, will the flexibility required for certification undermine attempts to institute parity of esteem of vocational and academic qualifications?
- What do we mean by "skill"? Is it different from a collection of competences? Should we insist on all those who obtain skill certification demonstrating ability to communicate a body of knowledge in a formal examination?

Theme II: The role of assessment and certification in the functioning of training and labour markets

The ideal system of vocational certification is one which identifies for the employer the individual who fits the employer's job requirements. If the college or work-based training has already provided the skills needed for a particular job, the employer saves valuable resources which would otherwise be spent on offering this training; the new employee is more productive and the employer recognises this by paying a premium (wage differential). This acts as a signal to potential trainees that investment of time and resources pays off, and they thus come forward for training. This, of course, is an idealised virtuous circle of certification, productivity, higher earnings and increased training effort that is very difficult to achieve in practice. Nevertheless, recognition of the fact that certification should attest to skills that the employer needs and values underlies much of the effort that colleges, examining bodies and governing authorities invest in certification.

The rapidly changing requirements of the labour market in advanced industrialised countries was analysed earlier. Some countries, whether as a conscious policy decision or because of the way their systems have evolved, do not provide for large-scale certification of specific occupational competences within the framework of the full-time education system. This is a view that can be justified on the grounds of the increasing relevance to modern industry and commerce of flexibility and adaptability of employees and a high level of general education. Other countries continue to offer certification in specific occupational areas but, increasingly, the requirements of flexibility and adaptability are being built into the design and assessment of such qualifications. It is possible that the former arrangement may be more suitable for countries with internal labour markets where firms expect to carry out training and updating of employees (notable examples are Japan and France), whereas countries with more active external labour markets tend to be associated with more occupationally specific certification.

However, the rapidly changing labour-market requirements of firms raise the important question of whether training for specific occupations is appropriate preparation for employment in advanced industrialised economies. Inevitably, certification is formulated on the basis of already established occupational patterns. By the time these have been institutionalised in large-scale certification arrangements, the occupations certified may no longer be needed. It may even be dysfunctional for an economy if the skills certified are modelled too closely on employers' requirements; employers themselves may be basing production on outmoded and inefficient patterns of division of labour, and the output of the certification process may merely help to perpetuate these inefficiencies. All countries must therefore find ways of resolving the problem of forward planning of certification of vocational competences so as not only to respond to industry's immediate needs but to ensure the provision of future skill requirements, which, by their nature, cannot be predicted with any accuracy.

OECD countries have developed a variety of strategies for confronting these problems. On the one hand, we have the approach based almost exclusively on laying a good foundation of general skills (Japan) and on the other, an approach which closely involves employer and employee organisations in drawing up training programmes and supplementing them with on-the-job training which ensures that requirements are close to the latest needs (Germany). In between, other interesting combinations of work-based and college-based certification have been developed (e.g. the Netherlands, Denmark). These options need to be explored in order to determine the best way of ensuring that certification is appropriate to both present and future skill needs.

It has already been mentioned that, ideally, employers signal their recognition of certification by paying a premium for certificated skills. A necessary condition is that certification should be transparent and perceived to be reliable. In a number of countries, notably those with national state-validated systems of certification, employee organisations have pressed for and obtained recognition in wage-grading systems of widely recognised vocational certification. The advantages of this are, briefly, greater incentives to individuals to invest in skills, and a good supply of well-qualified individuals. Disadvantages include to rigidities both in labour markets and in training systems where innovation or new certification may have to be negotiated with both employer and employee representatives. Nevertheless, working groups will need to weigh up whether the advantages of a good supply of qualified individuals (and avoidance of the "poaching" problem) outweigh the unavoidable rigidities.

What are the factors leading to employers – therefore individual trainees – valuing occupational certification? It is argued that recognition by employers of vocational competences is easier to achieve if the certification is perceived as reliable – that is, standard both over time and over the national or regional territory, if it is simple and easy to understand, yet conveys the type of information that the employer seeks. It is a great virtue of many systems of national occupational certification that standards of competence certified have been maintained over time – mainly through external examinations and control of syllabuses – and that employers have built up a "picture" of what the certificate attests by familiarity with the work of those who hold it. Inevitably, the need for reliability and simplicity conflicts with the need to adapt certification to dynamic labour markets. Countries have developed different ways to reconcile these conflicting demands.

It is not only on entry to working life that individuals need to be persuaded to invest in training. The advantages of certification systems which offer career progression throughout working life are explored elsewhere. Individuals are more likely to invest in initial training if they can see opportunities for progression beyond their first certificate. Again, these must correspond to employers' needs and offer realistic prospects of advancement. This means that the most successful systems of employee certification will thus be recognised in collective agreements while still allowing the employer discretion over whether or not to promote an employee who holds an appropriate qualification.

Questions debated by the working groups

- Is it in the longer-term interests of young people and of employers to train young people in one occupational skill area corresponding to employers' immediate skill needs?

- Do labour markets in advanced industrialised countries need young people with a good grounding of general education rather than training in specific occupational competences? Or both?

- Is it more appropriate for the latter to be offered in countries with predominantly internal labour markets (promotion and training within one company)?

- Is it more appropriate for the former to be offered in countries with predominantly external labour markets (employees move between employers)?

- Should certification be based upon a description of the competences required for current jobs, or should it seek to encourage the sorts of skills required by advanced industrialised economies in the longer term (flexibility, adaptability)?

- If employers are to "recognise" a certificate, it should not change too much over time. How can this requirement for stability be reconciled with the need to respond to employers' changing skill requirements?

- Which combinations of college-based and work-based training appear to reconcile these conflicting demands in the most satisfactory way?

- Collective agreements embodying wage differentials for recognised vocational qualifications encourage young people and older employees to invest time and resources in obtaining certification. Do these advantages outweigh the rigidities these agreements introduce into labour markets?

- What are the best ways of persuading adult employees to upgrade their skills? Which patterns of career progression within specific occupations work best?

- What are the best ways of keeping employers' needs for more advanced skills, and employees' investment of time and resources in upgrading their skills, roughly in balance?

Theme III: Portability and transferability of qualifications qualifications

One important aspect of transferability is whether, in national systems of certification, vocational certification should count equally with other general educational qualifications towards a certificate granting entry to higher education (university, polytechnical institute). While, traditionally, the two tracks (academic and vocational) have been kept separate, many countries now wish to award a single certificate giving access to jobs or higher education to all candidates. This means according equal weight to vocational and general academic studies. Such systems are seen as offering greater choice and flexibility to young people and, consequently, greater incentives to study. It is important for the credibility of training institutions that the certificates they award command widespread recognition in the labour market. Certificates awarded by new and unknown awarding bodies may take years to become established and recognised even though they certify a useful skill level.

One way of ensuring recognition across the whole of a national or regional territory is for the State to "underwrite" the certificate by providing quality assurance in the shape of a state-validated certificate. If, at the same time, whether by explicitly prohibiting other bodies from certificating skills or by some other use of monopolistic power, the State is effectively the only body validating vocational certificates, these will tend to gain wide acceptance in industry and commerce

– sometimes for want of anything better. The disadvantage of a single body is that there is little incentive to provide for relevance to industry's needs. An alternative pattern is for trade and industry bodies to set up and validate their own certificates for their own particular sector. This has the advantage of relevance but the disadvantage of being not easily transferable from one occupational sector to another. Ideally, it is in the interests of both employees and employers for certificates to be widely recognised across sectors and occupations as well as within them. A general education element common to all certificates can greatly assist transferability between sectors.

Progression within an occupation requires an extra dimension of a ladder of occupational qualifications and adequate opportunities for employees to pursue them. We should not forget the difficulty referred to above that employers are often reluctant to meet the cost of training employees to obtain certificates which would make it easier for them to move to another firm. One solution suggested in the United Kingdom is for employees to be required to pay back the cost of their training if they move jobs.

Even within one country, it may be useful for those awarding, gaining or trying to recognise different qualifications for an official classification system to provide equivalencies of a variety of different certificates. An example of this is the simple NVQ (National Vocational Qualification) framework of four levels in the United Kingdom.

Countries have often developed highly effective methods of evaluating the skills of immigrants and converting their certificates to a form which will be recognised in their new homeland, but EU countries have been slow to take any concrete action to promote the portability of vocational qualifications. At higher professional levels, some painfully negotiated agreements are now in place that allow professionally qualified workers (dentists, engineers) to compete on an equal footing with nationals of their new country. Yet progress has been slower with certificates of vocational competences. It is interesting to reflect on why this should be. Almost certainly, one reason are the very different types of certification awarded in the various EU countries at the vocational (craft) level as opposed to the higher professional level. This great diversity between systems of certification has been a major cause of the difficulty in reaching agreement on equivalencies in the EU.

Various solutions have been proposed: first, there was a proposal to set up a new "European" vocational qualification, but cost and the difficulty of obtaining agreement (especially from those who feel they already have a good system) has been a major deterrent. Second, negotiating agreement on multilateral recognition by national governments has been proposed, and steps towards this end have been taken by the European Centre for the Development of Vocational Training (CEDEFOP). Their approach has been to identify occupations or trades in the different EU countries and to bring together employer and employee representatives with other experts to list the certificates which attest to competence in that trade in each EU country. Undoubtedly, this could be of use to employers, but they would need a considerable amount of expertise in comparative vocational certification to make full use of it.

In practice, recent research carried out by task force of the EU among European employers has suggested that many employers of other EU nationals do not wish for more information or legislation on the harmonisation of vocational qualifications. Some employers had their own ways of assessing the competence of new employees from other EU States ("we give them a three-day trial period and if they are no good we let them go"). Overall, the view is that language differences still constitute a greater barrier to the mobility of workers in the EU than the lack of a harmonised system of vocational qualifications.

Questions debated by the working groups

- Should providers and planners aim to make vocational courses count towards a certificate leading to higher education in the same way that academic programmes do? Or should vocational certificates only give access to jobs and not to higher education?
- What is the best arrangement for ensuring widespread recognition of vocational certificates across sectors? What are the alternatives to the State acting as validating body? Can one national system of certification be sufficiently responsive?
- How is progression to higher levels of responsibility within an occupation best assured? What are the available models?
- Should there be classification systems to provide a national framework for qualifications offered locally or regionally?
- Should EU countries aim for a new common vocational certificate or will mutual recognition be sufficient to promote mobility of workers?

Theme IV: Implementing assessment, certification and validation validation

In schools, colleges, work places and workshops, many different "actors" contribute to the complex tasks of assessment leading to certification. Much debate revolves around who should do the assessing. Clearly, teachers and trainers are those who best know what students can do and should therefore make an important contribution to the assessment process. In some countries teachers set examination papers and mark others. Elsewhere, some teachers devise their own forms of assessment and mark their students' work themselves. Difficult problems of establishing reliable standards from one school or college to another arise from this practice, and "moderators" are frequently used to help iron out inconsistencies. Students often learn better when assessment is adjusted by the teacher to their individual aptitudes and this advantage should not be lost from view.

Employer and employee representatives also participate in the assessment process in some countries, which has the valuable effect of helping to ensure that assessment is reasonably relevant and informing those in industry and commerce of what is being taught and assessed in colleges. In some countries, work place supervisors also play a role. This can give rise to misgivings when these supervisors have themselves not been properly trained and do not fully understand their role. With proper training, as in Germany for example, this can also be a valid and motivating form of assessment. Whether the assessors are drawn from schools or industry or both, the need for consistent validation of standards is paramount. Students need to be given confidence that the certificate for which they have worked is of value, and a responsible validation body is one which uses the best professional practice to ensure that proper assessment procedures are observed at all times and that the standards certified remain as comparable as possible over time and over the different occupational sectors.

Often, the State is the best guarantor of standards over time, but there are examples of employer and employee representatives taking responsibility in some OECD countries and of independent bodies also fulfilling this function. One idea which does not seem to function well is that of a "market in qualifications": competing bodies strive to maximise the numbers of candidates paying to enter for certificates and tend to progressively lower standards!

Different sorts of learning require appropriate assessment, and practical skills will necessitate that practical tasks be observed and assessed. Many countries have considerable experience in assessing this sort of learning in a professional manner (the Netherlands, Switzerland – to name but a few). Such practical assessment can be more costly than the traditional short written test but is essential to underpin any worthwhile system of certification of vocational competence.

The problem of assessing the prior learning of experienced employees has already been discussed at length. Here we need to recall the need to assess skills already acquired rather than potential skills, to avoid imposing irrelevant requirements of academic education if that is going to prevent the employee receiving any certification. Prior learning can be assessed in a wide variety of ways – by project work, by self-assessment, as well as by more conventional methods.

Colleges and other institutions providing assessment of vocational competences are often faced with formidable logistical problems as a result of administering many modes of assessment for different types of students – full-time, part-time, part work-based, adults receiving accreditation of prior learning, or adults on updating and retraining courses. There is a need to consider the cost in time and resources of systems of assessment which are too fragmented and individualised. There are many advantages to establishing one framework for the assessment of all these different groups in order to benefit from economies of scale.

The advantages and disadvantages of assessment of modular units and of "pick 'n mix" systems have been spelt out above. While these can greatly benefit the learner, by being more flexible and allowing greater freedom of choice, employers have a more difficult task trying to understand such qualifications in terms of what the student can do. It was pointed out earlier that employers generally favour a simple certificate outlining the level and type of occupational skill acquired. If modules have to be listed in exhaustive detail, information overload can result and the qualification may not receive the recognition from employers that it deserves.

It can be recalled here that assessing competence on the basis of observation of an individual performing a task relies heavily on the assessor correctly interpreting the criteria laid down. Great variability can result from different interpretations of the criteria. The competences assessed do not necessarily add up to a skill – which may be assessed by more holistic methods: oral interview, continuous assessment over time. The competences may be backward-looking, to occupations as they were when the list of competences was drawn up, rather than as they are evolving. Competence-based systems of assessment can be very effective ways of certificating skills acquired by adult employees on the job but can limit young people to mechanical tasks and fail to develop all-round potential.

Questions debated by the working groups

- What should be the role of teachers in assessment? Of trainers? Of work place supervisors? Of employer and employee representatives?

- Do the advantages of allowing teachers and others to devise and mark their own assessments outweigh the disadvantages?

- Are moderators a sufficient safeguard of consistency of standards in teacher-based systems of assessment?

- Should the State take responsibility for validation or is there a case for handing responsibility to trade associations? And what about a free market in certificates?

- What are the best ways of assessing practical skills? Is a purely competence-based system of assessment adequate as a basis for assessing young people leaving school or college? Is it suitable for assessing competences acquired by adults "on the job"?

- Should colleges try to offer a wide variety of different types of assessment to cater to the needs of different client groups? Is such diversity unmanageable and should costs of assessment be controlled in some way so that teaching and learning do not suffer? Can assessment be too complex?

– Do the disadvantages of modular systems in obtaining employer recognition outweigh the advantages to learners of choice and flexibility? Are there ways of overcoming the problem of employer recognition?

– Are employers frequently reluctant to allow employees whom they have trained to obtain formal certification? If so, can ways be found to persuade employers to award certificates for in-house training which will be recognised on external labour markets?

PROBLEMS OF DEFINITION

by

Gabriel Fragnière
College of Europe, Bruges

INTRODUCTION

The combined dynamics of different political, technological, economic and social factors lead us to think that the issue of certification of professional qualifications, whether initial or acquired during one's career, has to be considered in an entirely new way in industrialised countries.

The political factors are linked to the globalisation of the economy and to a growing mobility of skilled workers in this world economy. With European integration and the prospects opened by the Maastricht treaty, the issues of vocational education, qualifications, certification and the skills market are now being examined in quite a new light.

The technological factors are linked to the continuing development of the means and methods of production of both goods and services, to the anticipated acceleration of these changes in the last decade of the century, and to their impact on the organisation of work, the transformation of tasks and functions, the development of further training in enterprises, and the restructuring of classifications and hierarchies within production systems. For this reason, one can no longer consider the problem of certification as simply an element of technical assessment of initial or acquired training. It is necessary, rather, to place certification within the overall context of factors of development determining life at work that will condition the role that this certification will play in setting active human resource policies in the future.

The new policies regarding human resources will themselves significantly change their orientation, moving from a logic of redistribution to one of investment. These new policies can no longer be satisfied with redistributing production profits to the work forces *downstream* in the economic process; on the contrary, they should develop policies *upstream* in the production process in order to guarantee and improve it. In fact, dealing with human resources consists of taking the appropriate measures in favour of living and working conditions to allow an optimal use of individual competences and their continued development. This in turn ensures competitive enterprises and the success of economic activity itself. Emphasis will therefore be placed more on the social investment of training and the valorisation of qualifications than on income redistribution. The certification of qualifications will thus take on a completely new role and its socio-economic impact will increase. For this reason it is impossible to discuss certification issues in an isolated manner. It is not certification itself which raises new questions but the changing socio-economic conditions in which it operates.

Furthermore, when one considers the ever-increasing role played by enterprises in further training activities, their growing influence on the formulation of initial training policies and the impact of these activities on occupational classifications and consequently on industrial relations and collective agreements, it is clear that new initiatives must be taken in this field, which may fundamentally transform the very nature of all policies affecting qualifications, including certification processes. This paper has been written taking into account these elements and attempts to propose some views concerning the main factors which will affect the development of certification processes, and to clarify related ideas.

Descriptions and analyses of the specific methods of certification as they are currently practised in OECD Member countries can be found elsewhere in this volume. The present text provides a general overview of some basic elements, with emphasis on the future goals and actors of certification. Rather than describing the way it presently functions, which in any case is being completely overhauled, it provides some indications of possible causes of future changes. This approach should facilitate the understanding of potential future orientations.

Furthermore, it is necessary to keep in mind the fact that certification is just one of the elements at work in the big race for new qualifications and competences that will affect the future prosperity of industrialised countries.

1. CERTIFICATION AND THE INTERVENTION OF PUBLIC AUTHORITIES

It is worthwhile to begin by questioning the reasons which justify an interest, if not an *obligation*, for national and even international public authorities such as the European Union to intervene in the field of certification, and this, independent of the initiatives which may result from the interplay of social actors or partners in industrial relations. There are five reasons:

– The first is to *guarantee the equality* of citizens in the framework of national employment markets, or freedom of movement of workers from larger multinational areas. Since everyone will be free to settle and work – that is, to assert the qualifications acquired through training and the individual competences of his personal experience – certification systems must not constitute a new form of discrimination between citizens of different regions or sectors within countries or between countries. It is therefore extremely necessary to establish transparency of existing certification systems and in some cases new certification measures. This is also necessary in order to recognise as soon as possible the value of the competences acquired through individual mobility. It is not a question of calling for the recognition of diplomas, in the sense understood by the EU, but rather the possibility of having one's experience valorised, especially if it is the result of mobility.

– The second reason comes from the need to establish rules for the normal *functioning of the skills market*. In fact, it is not possible to let market laws alone govern the field of qualifications and competences, because there can be many interests at stake behind the people directly concerned. On the one hand, there are the interests of the qualifications transmission systems – that means the institutions of initial and further training, the influence and the number of which are increasing. On the other hand are the interests of professional groups and enterprises where new competences are developing. Just as there are very specific rules at the economic level to ensure freedom of competition in an open market, so the same is true for the skills market. These rules are naturally more difficult to identify in a world undergoing dramatic change. While it is impossible to define in advance and in an exhaustive way all emerging new skills, it is necessary to have at hand a common means of identifying and recognising them.

– The third reason is a corollary of the second, but viewed in a dynamic perspective. Since the new "knowledge-based economy" now taking shape will radically transform the economic well-being of industrialised countries, with human competences thus becoming the main economic resource of the future, it is logical that public authorities, concerned with implementing the basic structures of the future economy, should be directly interested in these resources and their valorisation. The changes in qualifications, together with the recognition of their existence, and their impact on the new classification structures of functions and tasks – all this cannot be usefully controlled unless the observation of the changes extends to the certification process by which the new qualifications are formally confirmed within the new structures. As certification policies and economic policies are so closely linked, it is difficult to imagine developing one without taking an interest in the other.

– Fourthly, if certification can be considered a form of "quality label" attached to the qualifications and new competences of human resources, it seems evident that the authorities responsible for the overall equilibrium of the economy need to ensure some level of quality in the labelling process. This would explain the desire for some kind of control, mainly through transparency of certification procedures.

– Qualitative control of procedures can also offer a means to maintain very accurate information concerning quantitative changes in qualifications and competences, and thereby meet the requirements of the authorities responsible for the supply and renewal of human resources necessary to the economic well-being of the community. The quantitative renewal of skilled personnel, in other words the diploma holders, in several sectors of the economy and in very specific occupations, not only depends on the importance of the infrastructure available (number of places in schools, training personnel, etc.) but also on the nature of the selection process and the certification methods. The problems of quantity and quality therefore converge. Questions concerning the long-term planning of human resources and, in the longer term, the implementation of policies for the immigration of skilled foreign labour, are closely related and must be dealt with head-on, in order to resolve domestic shortages in this area.

These reflections simply underline the importance of a problem which is often only considered from a technical and methodological standpoint. It is for this very reason that public authorities cannot remain indifferent to what is happening in the area of certification.

2. PROBLEMS RAISED BY DEFINITIONS

From the outset it is necessary to define a certain number of terms in order to situate more accurately the questions to be tackled and to avoid possible confusion at the time of reading.

All of the concepts used here can be found in the *Thésaurus européen de l'éducation*[1] which provides a translation of the main terms in the field of education, in every language of the European Union. However, inferences are deliberately made from definitions contained in this thesaurus in order to give these concepts a more practical dimension. This has had to be done not only to take into account the most recent changes in the very use of the terms but also to make constructive proposals in this area, with a view to developing new instruments to understand and control a new situation.

In fact, the certification problem, considered as a field of action for the public authorities, naturally looks to traditional concepts from the education and training world. Nevertheless, these should be extended to other areas of application, such as the work world, the employment and competitivity market, where the use of words should take new factors into account to be fully operational. The concept of competitiveness, for instance, should be applied to the situation of the individual in the labour market and to problems faced by firms in the national and international economy, as well as to issues concerning regions and countries in the world economy. Its meaning cannot remain univocal but must be extended to take into account the specific circumstances of each situation where there is competition.

Furthermore, it is necessary to consider the change affecting the fields where these terms are used. Therefore, in order to cover totally this new reality in a changing training and work world, the contents must be clearly specified and, above all, the sense in which these concepts will be used.

Certification

Certification is an official and "formal" confirmation of acquired knowledge or qualifications, a ratification of success achieved in a training course or exam. It is a "formal" act of social, administrative or legal confirmation, thus implying force of sanction, ratification.

As a result, it is important to emphasize that certification, in the form of a certificate or a diploma, is an instrument with a real social and economic power, the scope of which extends beyond the training system. Certification has in fact a social and economic significance, independent of the institutions which grant it. It is a process which gives the individual – who now has "certified" qualifications at his disposal – a means of action protected by law which may have a high market value. It is therefore understandable that people or professional groups attach importance to the control of certification processes. One also sees how much it is necessary for public authorities to control the procedures by which institutions are entitled to "certify" qualifications. Certification is in fact an act of power. In this sense, it should be clearly distinguished from assessment.

Assessment

This is an action of evaluation and control which concerns the training itself or its results but does not necessarily imply a formal, official sanction. Assessment is a form of judgement which may concern as much the student as the trainer or teacher, as much the training methods as the results; it may have as its sole purpose, for example, to help the trainee to better understand what he does and thus provide pedagogical assistance for him to continue his studies. It may also serve to evaluate the quality of training in order to improve it. There are many possible assessment approaches. However, none of them has a purpose outside the education or training system. Their only social or economic purpose is their judgement of the system itself.

There is sometimes confusion between the assessment act of a training institution and its entitlement to grant a formal certification to the students or trainees who through it have attended a complete training programme. It is deduced that the value of training certification granted by the institution depends directly on the institution's assessment; this is the origin of confusion between assessment by the institution and certification policy. The two must be carefully distinguished, as will be seen later in the paper when the respective responsibilities of professional groups and States are analysed.

This is the reason why it is necessary to emphasize that certification is *exclusively* viewed here as a formal act of recognition and validation of training in the form of *individual diplomas or professional certificates*, which is seen in terms of its economic and social scope and not in those of the accreditation policies of the institutions themselves. One must also take into account that, while certification is always formal, there are also less formal modes of recognising acquired competences. These can be grouped together under the title valorisation.

Valorisation

This takes on increasing importance in the area of further training because valorisation concerns more directly the so-called "training acquisition" added to basic training. This valorisation is, first of all, a social recognition which, as its name suggests, emphasizes the economic, social and/or market *value* of a qualification acquired by an individual outside of the strictly formal systems where certification prevails.

Yet the economic consequences of valorisation can be important. It naturally plays a key role in numerous collective negotiations, mainly when the issue is *valorisation* or *revalorisation* of certain occupational categories. Naturally, valorisation must be prepared through a specific process which implies a sort of examination in the form of a "skills appraisal", to some extent similar to a certification process and which may be formalised if necessary. The function and conditions of such skills appraisals are often negotiated between social partners or are even the subject of an accord, such as the agreement recently reached in France.[2] However, they do not necessarily lead to a revision of the formal certification processes in countries.

It is important to point out the difference that can exist between these valorisation agreements negotiated between social partners to improve work quality, and the measures taken by public authorities that result in a formal certification. In any case, a clear distinction between these two concepts of valorisation and certification will enable a better identification of the actors involved.

The contents of certification

It is also important in this reflection to consider carefully the subject or content of certification. While systems often differ in form and procedure across countries, all relate to common contents – that is, the aptitudes required by specific professions. These contents, and the concepts in which they are expressed – knowledge, know-how, qualifications, skills – must also be defined at this stage.

It is important to emphasize that concepts must be considered as part of a whole. It is not possible to talk of knowledge or qualification or skill, viewing them as purely abstract notions. Insofar as certification is considered an official act of social recognition of the concrete aptitudes of a profession, it only applies to an ensemble. This paper therefore looks at knowledge, qualifications and competences in the plural.

Sets of knowledge

Sets of knowledge – one can also use the term understanding – is what one acquires through learning. It is exclusively of a cognitive order, cumulative, and able to take place at different levels of abstraction. Knowledge means knowing what things are or how they work. The knowledge at issue here has a high degree of objectivity, sociability (it is shared by many), as well as transferability.[3] The transfer of knowledge is in fact the main role played by education and training structures.

Know-how

This refers to the knowledge used in specific activity processes. The English expression "know-how" clearly indicates that it is a matter of knowledge enabling an individual to act on things he knows. It is also defined as an ability to solve practical problems in an appropriate way. This power to act is a possession, something one has objectively and can also pass on. Know-how has a double potential: individual and social. It can be characterised as an ensemble of knowledge, experience and also techniques (in the sense of an activity process) accumulated by individuals or a society, which can be exploited and placed at other people's disposal, free of charge or against payment. Thus, it is possible to have one's expertise valorised in market terms. Know-know can be bought or sold, in the form of patents or diplomas. But what most characterises expertise – and this is what distinguishes it from competences – is the fact that it is easily and objectively transferable – which explains its central place in training – and marketable. An important aspect of expertise, at a certain level, is to determine who owns it: the individual or the institution, particularly in the case where a company made acquisition of this expertise possible. There is an essential problem here in estimating the profitability of investment in training. Insofar as the trained individual may leave, taking with him the specialised knowledge he has acquired, is the investment not a total loss? But this touches on other aspects of the skills market, notably the definition of ownership over acquired knowledge, which is beyond the scope of this analysis.

Qualifications

Qualifications are the ensemble of knowledge or know-how necessary for the *accomplishment of a specific task.* When defining qualifications, it is important to point out that they are determined by the task fulfilled rather than by the subjective acquisition of the individuals who have assimilated them. The qualification notion supposes a direct usefulness. Qualifications are necessary to do something very specific. All of the individuals likely to participate in this activity should thus acquire the same qualifications. The concept of qualification unquestionably encompasses something objective and universal. It is therefore possible, in principle, to define qualifications *a priori,* to describe them according to their purpose and to outline their shape before they are acquired or transferred.

It is also possible to determine the amount of qualifications necessary, expressed in the number of qualification holders or persons qualified to carry out certain tasks. It is subsequently possible to establish some principles for planning of qualifications production based on estimates of needs and, if the case arises, to consider qualification deficits in view of foreseeable technological trends.

There is a direct relationship between technological change and the transformation of qualifications. Technology affects directly (but not necessarily) task contents; on the one hand it implies a work reorganisation, on the other a new definition of qualifications related to the new tasks. For this reason it is possible to anticipate in abstract the changes in qualifications, independently of what is happening in the training systems themselves.

It is also for this reason that those training systems which are not in direct contact with the world of work and are not aware of changing qualifications have become out of date and can no longer transmit the required qualifications. In this case, certification risks formalising useless qualifications. There must always be agreement and mutual adaptation between qualifications and tasks.

It also explains why, in a changing world, qualifications users – companies – attempt to control as closely as they can the contents of the certification process, in order to diminish as much as possible the divide between the formal qualifications of the training system and the concrete qualifications required by real tasks of the work place. This progressive swing of responsibility, far from the more formal approach of the public authorities, is full of future possibilities, and it is necessary that the authorities take these into account. We will come back to this point when talking of actors. However, it is important, at this level, to distinguish these so-called objective and sociably definable qualifications from another issue: that of competences.

Competences

These are composed by the *individual* and, one would almost think, *subjective* ability to use one's qualifications, know-how and knowledge to accomplish something. In fact, there are no "objective" competences capable of being defined independently of the individuals in which they are embodied. There are no competences in and of themselves; there are only competent people.

This has a direct influence on the recognition of these competences and their transferability. Whereas it is possible to define a qualification often "required" *a priori* to fulfil a task (qualification is defined in relation to what must be done in an action system), the idea of competence has a not-expressed reference to the individuals in charge of it. Competences cannot be measured independently of the individuals who possess them. One only talks of competences in relation to knowledge in the case of knowledge assimilated by the individual, often even developed by himself.

It is the reason why, when discussing what the French call *compétences transversales*, the English "core qualifications" or the Germans *Schlüssel Qualifikationen* ("key qualifications"), there is a regrettable confusion between qualifications and competences. *Compétences transversales* are exactly those related to the individual, to his behaviour and his specifically personal abilities. They do not define gestures or know-how directly and objectively linked to a very specific task. The French word *compétences transversales* is the most precise, as it points out that abilities are not objectively defined by the object of professional action but by the agent's individual behaviour. The German and French languages in this case use the notion of qualification mistakenly, since it is actually a matter of competence.

Whereas knowledge and qualifications are the result of a training activity or a course of study – even when autonomous or individual – competences are "always" the outcome of experience. Competences, to be recognised as such, must show within and through an activity. It will be seen later that competences which originate in and are acquired through experience are gradually formalised through a very complex process and are transformed into transferable qualifications. But in principle, they are only the outcome of individual experience. A trainee repeating his lessons during an examination shows knowledge and qualifications in simply reciting or doing what he has learned; however, he shows his individual competences when he does it "his way", when his personal style shows through in his qualifications and knowledge. We pass from knowledge and qualifications to the demonstration of competences through action and experience. It is not possible to disembody competences since they do not exist without the human being who possesses them.

A skills market, therefore, is nothing more than a labour market; it is impossible to create it in the same way as a patents or certificates market. The market of competences is a market of the work of individuals.

Concluding remarks

These definitions, and the distinctions they imply, lead us to understand that although it is easy to establish a formal system of certification of knowledge and competences (and even of know-how, insofar as we wish to estimate its market value) – openly justifiable in the view of the public and clearly delimited from the viewpoint of the legal systems – it is much more difficult to do so for individual competences. Competences objectivisation cannot be done without active participation of the individual holders. Hence, one can see the importance of carefully analysing the way labour markets function and the role that professional groups play in guaranteeing the defence of the competences themselves.

Furthermore, it is important to make the distinction between the setting up of a *formal* certification system related to knowledge, qualifications and know-how, and an *informal* system for recognising individual competences. Both are necessary. It seems in fact that the intervention of public authorities balances these two needs.

3. THE OCCUPATIONAL WORLD IN A CHANGING SOCIETY

The public authorities are one of the actors influencing the certification process. It is therefore useful to know their position in relation to other agents and structures in the field. Partners exist, occupying well-established places which differ from one country to another and are influenced by educational and occupational traditions resulting from the interplay of interests during the historical development of national societies. Certification is currently evolving in an occupational world undergoing dramatic changes.

It is not possible to describe here all aspects of this transformation. However, it is good to keep in mind, when approaching the more specific problem of certification, the framework and the system of interactions (socio-economic, political and occupational) in which the present certification systems are evolving. What follows is a brief systemic analysis of the occupational world to clarify some specific processes.

When speaking about a particular profession such as that of engineer, electrician, salesman, accountant, physician, etc., we introduce five different elements, often implicit, which constitute the "sub-system" of a profession. They may be described as follows.

A profession is, first of all, a *specific function* within the production system, whether in goods or services, or in the socio-economic system in general. One knows what a physician does and one can easily distinguish his function from that of an opera singer or a lawyer. This function evolves with changes in the work organisation and the distribution of tasks among the various professions. Technology plays an essential if not determining role here. Professions evolve over time (it is a long way from the time when surgery was done by barbers using their razors as bistouries, to today's highly restrictive and reserved milieu of experts) and people's tasks are defined differently according to societies. In Europe, for example, the specific area of nurses' work activity often varies from country to country.

Each certification system must therefore take into account the definition of the occupation through its specific function in order to confirm, usefully and formally, the required qualifications. The mobility of skilled workers will surely lead to conflict between different conceptions at a time when the impact of technology is considerably transforming traditional definitions. It is therefore useful to know that this first aspect of occupation is currently quite uncertain, at least for the majority of existing professions, on which this technology has a direct impact.

Secondly, a profession implies a *coherent set of qualifications* or a *qualifications profile*; these sets of knowledge and know-how guarantee that their holder is able to fulfil the task he has been attributed in the traditional work division. These qualification sets evolve over time and according to the circumstances, and depend on changes in the tasks (through technology and work organisation) and training systems. In most cases these sets are defined *a priori* and constitute the minimum qualifications to be initially acquired. Certification systems are especially concerned with this qualifications set; to be a certified professional means that one has acquired the qualifications required by the occupational definition.[4]

This system works quite well in most cases of initial training. On the other hand, systems are less adapted when further training leads to significant changes in the qualification profile on which the occupational definition is based. The formal approach then becomes more and more deficient.

Thirdly, when we talk of a profession, we accept that a *formal training system* inevitably exists, serving simultaneously as a structure for the transfer of required qualifications (preparation for a profession) and as a path of entry to the profession through the certification of minimum qualifications (selection system). In fact, this training system is generally the main agent responsible for certifying qualifications and guaranteeing the quality. But as it also serves as a path of entry to the profession (with access sometimes very exclusive), this system often holds a considerable power of selection and control over the profession itself. In most cases, in fact, the power of certification implies a control over the profession. This is usually exercised through the formal training system.

The comparison of aggregated descriptions of vocational training systems such as the studies undertaken by CEDEFOP on the member states of the European Union, for example, do not always allow us to understand how, within these systems, each profession often has its own certification system with very specific procedures and policies, and which does not always give the results which normally should be coherent with the overall structures. These differences from one profession to another within the framework of an apparently common system are due to the level of autonomy of the vocational training and certification system in relation to the social structures of the profession. These will be called its fourth dimension.

A profession also implies, and perhaps above all, an *organised social group* which performs several functions. First, it is a system of socio-professional identification of individuals, of defence of the profession's social status, sometimes of control over the practice of this profession, and generally of the power of this profession over its members and in society at large. People often confuse the defence of the group's interests *vis-à-vis* third parties or society in general with the exercise of a professional power in economic and political life. Each profession clearly has its own policy which will be felt more or less strongly according to the type of organisation, the size of the social group it represents and the status of its professional function in society, which can be measured by its "degree of indispensability" or the extent of its monopoly. In this way the medical association has incontestable power over its members and society, much more so than could be hoped for by an association of shopkeepers, a union of craftsmen or skilled workers, an association of building companies, a society of computer science engineers or the alumni association of a highly specialised school. It is easy to see that the power of each of these associations varies according to the type of economic development and circumstances as well as regional structural features.

However, it is at the level of their relationship with the formal system of training and control of the certification process that professional organisations most openly exercise power over their members, because this is the stage in which they select and/or eliminate members and can also influence government policies on opening up or closing professions. A Malthusian attitude of a particular profession can lead to serious labour shortages in certain sectors of human resources. However, very lax opening can, on the contrary, lead to the devaluation of certain functions which, no longer attractive to young people, will eventually not be renewed. Analysis of this power of professional organisations leads one to realise the important role played by certification methods and processes in the relation between quality and quantity of human resource development.

Finally, each profession has a corresponding type of *career profile* that conditions three main aspects: rising income based on social status (a very motivating power); advancement in the hierarchy and power system; and the nature of the acquisition of individual competences through experience which, beyond formal qualifications, form a more or less exact and coherent picture of what one wishes to become in choosing a particular profession. There is thus also a non-formal type of certification, what we will call the informal valorisation of professions through a career. It is necessary to know the real power holders to understand all the consequences.

Structural dynamics

It is obvious that these five dimensions in the definition of professions are not static elements. They evolve dynamically and interactively, and their relative importance will depend on the way that each of these elements can influence the others. The pace of technological change transforms the first and second dimensions with an impact on the third – the formal training system – taking into account the relative autonomy of the latter, both in the work environment (school-based or company training) and in the professional organisation (the role of the State in establishing programmes or the role of professional associations). Finally, it is obvious that labour market demand will be decisive for the group's development (strong demand decreases its selectivity) and above all for career advancement.

It is therefore worthwhile to consider the issue of selection, and consequently certification, in relation to these changes. This certification will vary in nature, purpose and type of responsibility, depending on labour market trends as well as the real or perceived power of the professional social group. However, it is clearly the nature of the career which largely determines the extent of change possible in individual competences and most openly creates conditions of competitiveness in each profession or between the same professions in different countries. Obviously, the skills of a computer engineer will change much more quickly than the skills of a legal clerk.

As these variants are linked to countries' historical economic and industrial development, their culture and education system, one can expect great diversity across OECD countries and by profession. Insofar as this approach is useful to analyse countries and their possible reaction to the opening of the skills market, it helps one see that it is impossible to envisage a standardised certification system.

4. FROM "OFFICIAL" QUALIFICATIONS TO "REAL" COMPETENCES

Any analysis of the qualifications required for a profession must start with a description of the formal qualifications acquired during initial training, which on the whole corresponds to what is expected from the individuals who will carry out the function assumed by this profession within the system. In this sense, it is exact to say that certification – the culmination of a complete training programme – contains the definition of the occupation itself. In terms of qualifications, an individual *is* in fact what his diploma officially *says* he is.

However, knowledge and know-how do not stop at the initial training stage. The individual who works usually responds to new situations and experiences of practical life, and acquires attitudes, know-how and patterns of behaviours resulting more and more from experience and less and less from initial knowledge and know-how. His/her real professional competence is built during the stages of his/her career. In this way, it can be said that, in terms of competences, an individual *is* what he has really *done*, what he has *acquired*. This process can be schematically described as follows.

The initial *formal professional qualification* (*FPQ*) is a set of *qualifications acquired* through training (*aq*), which changes over the years through the acquisition of additional or supplementary qualifications *(sq)*. These may be achieved either through formal supplementary training, possibly even leading to partial additional certifications, or through the accumulation of experiences bringing an informal, practical *experiential competence (ec)* and gradually leading to an individualised profile of final qualifications and competences. This can be referred to as *real professional competence* (*RPC*) and does not always resemble the formal profile established by the initial certification. Here, there may be as many acquired qualifications *(aq)* disappearing from lack of use – although know-how survives thanks to "doing" and the activity rather than simply "knowing" – as new experiences appearing that no certification process can formalise because they are absolutely individual.

The following diagram illustrates this process:

Time 1 Certification	Time 2 ->	Time 3 ->	Time 4 ->	Time n Valorisation
aq	aq	–	ec	ec
aq	aq	aq	–	–
aq	aq	aq	aq	aq
aq	–	ec	ec	ec
aq	ec	ec	–	ec
aq	–	ec	ec	ec
etc.				
FPQ Certification	FPQ + ec ->	FPQ + ec ->	ec + FPQ ->	RPC Valorisation

Source: G. Fragnière for the OECD.

Each individual in a job moves progressively from a formal professional qualification (FPQ) sanctioned by an objective certification, or at least common to all the members of the profession in a given country, to real professional competence (RPC). This is completely individual, since it is always an interactive mix of added qualifications and competences acquired through experience, and only has an objective value for the company in which it was acquired. Nevertheless, this real professional competence (RPC) escapes, by its very nature, the starting certification or any other manner of certifying formal complementary training, because it is due more to practical experience than training. It can only be the subject of valorisation, which is something different altogether.

The issue faced by large economic areas such as the European Union – in the context of the internal market and, above all, in relation to the rapid and dramatic changes currently felt by every labour system due to technological development – is one of organising a human resources market that is mainly composed of individuals whose real competences are neither interchangeable nor "objectivable". Methods of recognition and valorisation must be found that do not try to imitate the principles of a redundant formal certification process but ensure the functioning of the competences market so that it is: *a)* fair, *b)* competitive, and *c)* transparent.

The key question is how to establish an objective system of control and assessment of competences, keeping in mind that these are "individual" and valorised only inside the companies where they are applied. How can formal certification be replaced by an objective, non-formal process of determining competences on which the labour market of many different countries will be based? Is it possible to design a process of valorising of real competences that could be common to several countries and "subsidiary" to their formal systems?

5. CERTIFICATION AND/OR VALORISATION OF COMPETENCES

In a formal training process, qualifications are subject to a precise definition in relation to the final profile of qualifications necessary to practise a given profession. This can be called the "qualitative" dimension of the profession. In this case, qualifications are determined and acquired before being used or applied.

In the work place, competences are developed from experience only. Furthermore, it is sometimes impossible to know in advance which competences will be acquired. There is consequently a path or process of subjective skills revelation which, for the purposes of this paper, can be called the path to skills objectivisation.

An attempt must now be made to define and clarify this. The path is composed of five stages:

a) *Skills identification.* This is a process of awareness, first on the part of the individual and gradually by the firm in which he works, that the activity undertaken and the practice acquired have given rise to one or several new competences. An innovative learning process has taken place concerning a specific function of a given profession: the invention of a new process, the linking of previously separate activities, the unplanned implementation of a new technology, etc. This identification of new skills from experience requires an ability not only to learn by oneself but also to be aware of the learning activity which has taken place. The process is also favoured by new management ideas advising the establishment of "self-learning organisational structures" and the participation of each individual in the reorganisation of the work process.[5] This identification of the new competence is still very spontaneous and individual, almost intuitive. However, it is characterised by a very active participation of workers and their direct supervisors, foremen and team leaders. The discovery is naturally closely linked to the type of work organisation, technology choice and the management of production itself. So these new competences develop and are identified in workshops and core groups – that is, within company production units. There is no need to emphasize the considerable scope for innovation that exists within small and medium firms.

b) *Competences recognition.* This is the art of making competences transparent once one has become aware of them. It consists of describing them in such a way that the group is able to speak of and transmit them. This stage is an initial conceptualisation of the competences developed and acquired by one or several individuals. Whereas during the first stage, knowledge could hardly be distinguished from practice, the conceptualisation of a new competence allows a more objective and scientific knowledge. The competence remains embodied in the individual, but it is possible to understand its contents. From that moment on, it is possible, at the company level, to elaborate a definition and anticipate its application and management in different production groups.

c) *Competences formalisation.* As soon as conceptual language is able to isolate a human process and practice into categories of qualified activity, it is possible to describe and define this competence and emphasize and valorise it in terms of knowledge, know-how, as well as objective behaviour. This objectivisation is necessary so that the skill can be transferred from one individual to another and from one team to another in the context where this competence is applied. In general, this formalisation of competences is done in the framework of a definition of tasks within the company and becomes a "home-grown process", a way of linking a specific type of work organisation to a specific culture. It is possible, at this stage, to pass from the level of simple recognition of individual competences to the recognition of company know-how, which can from then on be commercialised. Naturally, there is no such thing as "qualifications patents" forbidding imitation or transfer of competences between firms. However, it is possible for a company that has developed specialised know-how to benefit on the open market, with the competence of its own human resources as a special asset. But it is necessary to go through this formalisation stage so that the existence of these competences becomes a commercial argument. Nevertheless, the company does not yet entirely control the know-how, since this may disappear if the individuals possessing it leave. The purchase and sale of competences through the mobility of qualified staff is part and parcel of this large competences market that the industrialised countries wish to encourage. "Head hunters", who know how to pick out these new competences and identify them in the individuals whose profile they are looking for, openly contribute to the organisation of such a market. Yet it is precisely in becoming fully aware of some of the uncontrollable aspects of this competences market that we generally pass to the following stage.

d) *Competences standardisation.* This stage occurs when competences, formalised by the market, are gradually transformed into models imitable and transferable between individuals. It is perhaps the stage where competences, having become widespread in the practice of a profession, are gradually identified with new qualifications and fulfil the same role – that is, what it is absolutely necessary to know in order to perform a very specific function. Competences that are invented and spontaneously developed become, through standardisation, the object of imitation by the entire occupational world. It is at this level that professional organisations, owing to the pressure of change in practice, begin a redefinition of their profiles of specialisation to reinforce the image of their profession. The example of computer science is perhaps the most vivid: starting from basic-language knowledge and software considered to be simple commercial products, the basic qualifications of the profession have gradually come to be defined as the mastery of these different languages.

e) *Competences valorisation.* This is the stage in which the acquisition by individuals of specific competences is institutionally recognised and taken into account in the structuring of jobs and functions. At this level, the competence arising from practice is recognised as an acquired qualification. This skills valorisation plays an important part in the reform of occupational classifications, in job and salary structures, and in the process of continuing and further training programmes within firms. There is a lot of discussion about the need for "qualifying training" programmes – that is, training activities leading to a valorised competence. At this particular stage, the interplay of social partners, of negotiations between employers and unions, is significant and decisive. It generally precedes the stage which implemented the regulation of competences and qualifications.

f) *Regulation of competences/qualifications.* Regulation recognises the necessity to make these special competences compulsory for all those who practice the profession. It is a return to the traditional formalisation of the occupation and is the specific level of certification – that is, determining the profession *a priori* through basic training confirmed by a diploma or certificate. At this level, the public authorities confirm, through various regulations, the changes that have occurred in the organisation of companies' work and culture, in the labour market and in negotiations between the social partners.

The processes of qualifications development

Today we have a better understanding of how occupational qualification systems work, as well as the relation between informal experience and the formal approach of regulations. While the *informal* path described above is that of practice and development of competences and qualifications in one's professional life, the path of *formal* training processes takes an opposite direction, starting from what is regulated (in terms of occupational profile) and who teaches, certifies and then practises it. The order is completely reversed. In the table below, the informal system of occupational practice approaches the qualifications issue, moving from stage a) to stage f). The formal training system starts from stage f) and the remaining practice stages are expected to follow more or less automatically.

The first important observation is that different actors intervene at each stage. They should be identified now, to enable a better understanding of who intervenes and in which context.

Identifying these stages of qualifications development allows one to understand easily the level of technological and work organisation factors which depend on the basic management of production processes – that is, the individual firms taken as productivity and competitivity agents – and to understand the role played by professional organisations as described in Section 3 above, as managers and defenders of the interests of given professions. Often the transition between these different stages depends on the existence of strong professional structures and institutions. It is therefore important to point out that, in an international labour market, changes are increasingly difficult to predict because they are directly conditioned by factors over which public authorities have no influence. A coherent approach to the issues is preferable but, first of all, it is necessary to know what causes the incoherence observed.

Stages	Actors
a) Identification	Individual worker Production organisation Core groups
b) Recognition	Core groups Foreman Production engineers Management
c) Formalisation	Companies Know-how market Industrial processes or Services producers
d) Standardisation	Professional associations
e) Valorisation	Companies Union and employer associations (collective agreements, competence market)
f) Regulations-certification	Public authorities Training institutions Professional groups

Source: G. Fragnière for the OECD.

This analysis also leads to the conclusion that the institutions of basic training – responsible for certification and formal qualification profiles – must keep a close contact with the work place so that they are not overtaken by developments they are unaware of. In most cases, obsolete training programmes, the main cause of qualifications shortages, are due to lack of contact between training institutions and the work world. The only exceptions are Germany and other countries that rely on a dual system, recognising the important role played by professional chambers in the determination of training programmes. Therefore, the solution would be to establish a link between the procedures described above, whereby the informal "routes" passing from a) to f) are more directly connected with the formal "routes" passing from f) to a). What we have called the path to competence objectivisation, which follows that of practical experience, should be called the "path of qualifications transformation". It should start with formal diplomas and gradually integrate individual competences that have been added. The result would be a structure of initial and continuing vocational training systems with less formalism and more participation. But this requires the involvement of all the actors concerned.

NOTES

1. Conseil de l'Europe and Commission des Communautés Européennes (1991), *Thésaurus européen de l'éducation*, Office des publications officielles des Communautés Européennes, Luxembourg.

2. National interprofessional agreement of 3rd July 1991, concluded between employers and trade unions, concerning training and occupational proficiency.

3. It is useful to make the distinction here between transportability of knowledge or competences, which will be considered at the time of geographical displacements within the outline of mobility, and transferability of competences allowing the transfer from one professional milieu to another. See on the matter Rhys Gwyn (1990), "Formation et transfert des compétences", in *L'Europe des Compétences*, Commission des Communautés Européennes, Secrétariat d'État entrusted with Occupational Training, Presses Interuniversitaires Européennes, Brussels, pp. 79-90.

4. There are several research programmes or observatories at the EU which attempt to analyse developments taking place in the area of qualifications. It is interesting to mention those which aim to understand the dynamics of the situation rather than simply present a static table of correspondences. Among them we distinguish the EPOQUAL project (Emerging Patterns of Qualifications and Learning) from the programme EUROTECNET which proposes a very precise technology that can be adapted to each occupational definition.

5. See Marcelle Strootbants (1993), *Savoir-faire et compétences au travail*, Editions ULB, Université libre de Bruxelles. See also Barry Nynan (1991), *Promouvoir l'aptitude à l'auto-formation – Perspectives européennes sur la formation et le changement technologique*, EUROTECNET, TFRH, Presses Interuniversitaires Européennes, Brussels.

PROBLEMS OF IMPLEMENTING ASSESSMENT AND CERTIFICATION

by

Sheila Clarke
Consultant
and
Ron Tuck
Her Majesty's Chief Inspector
The Scottish Office Education Department, Edinburgh

This paper was presented to the Porto conference plenary session on 30 October 1992. Since the paper was written, developments have occurred in Scotland (as indeed elsewhere) to address many of the issues at the heart of this paper. In March 1994 the Scottish Office Education Department (SOED) set out its plans, in the publication *Higher Still: Opportunity for All*, for a reformed post-16 education system. The SOED is also making progress in the reform of the further education lecturer qualification.

INTRODUCTION

This paper aims to clarify several aspects of the implementation of certification. It is impossible, of course, to discuss implementation without reference to the other seminar themes. What VOTEC (Vocational and Technical Education and Training) objectives are we seeking to achieve? These objectives vary from country to country but include some if not all of the following:

- a unified education and training system, or at least parity of esteem;

- the development of basic skills/knowledge as well as specific competences;

- pathways to higher education as well as employment;

- demanding but attainable targets for all;

- training that is relevant to employers' needs;

- flexible delivery including work place learning, open learning, and validation of prior learning experience;

- effective teaching methods;
- efficiency.

These objectives are not straightforward. They engender tensions or dichotomies, three of which will be briefly explained here:

- the "academic/vocational divide" (with particular reference to the issue of competences);
- internal and external assessment;
- centralisation and decentralisation.

1. LEARNING OUTCOMES AND COMPETENCES

Before turning to the first of these issues, there is a question of definition to address: the distinction between learning outcomes and skills. An *outcome* is a clearly defined end-product of a learning process (for example, "knowing how bacteria develops in kitchens" or "understanding the implications of the Maastricht Treaty"). A *competence* is the ability to perform an actual occupational role (for example, "preventing the growth of bacteria in kitchens").

By definition, competence is therefore a particular kind of outcome which focuses on the ability to do something in a real context, rather than the mere possession of knowledge or a skill. It should be noted that the use of the term outcomes, in the sense indicated here, allows the specification of knowledge separately rather than requiring that knowledge be embedded in competence statements, although the strategy of embedding must also be used.

2. THE ACADEMIC/VOCATIONAL DIVIDE

Academic or general education is often seen in opposition to vocational training, from the viewpoint of methods and approaches. Vocational training is increasingly based on competences; academic education is often defined in terms of syllabus inputs but, at best, is outcome-based. In Scotland, as in other countries, there are many examples of school and higher education programmes devised to specify the learning targets by reference to a criteria.

While academic programmes are located in educational institutions, vocational training is more likely to be located in the work place. Academic education is relatively stable over time; vocational education and training requires regular updating.

Those involved in vocational education can view the general education sector as being divorced from the real world of work and occupational skills, and unresponsive to changing needs. Those responsible for general education see vocational education as being concerned with behavioural results to the detriment of educating the person as a whole, and they doubt the capacity of the work place to assure a good level of education.

How can this divide be bridged? One way forward might be to conceptualise education and training as a continuum rather than as a dichotomy (see Figure 1).

This continuum runs from theoretical and abstract learning to that which is usefully applied to employment. Both of these points on the continuum, and all those in between, have their place, depending on the purposes of learning. While it is easy to agree on the virtues of applied learning, it must also be recognised that abstract learning plays a role in the development of underlying knowledge which may translate into competence (as defined in Section 1 above) at a later stage of the learner's development.

At the centre of the continuum is general vocational education (National Vocational Qualifications in the United Kingdom, Tech Prep in the United States, the new school-based programmes in Sweden, and certain National Certificate Awards in New Zealand). General vocational education draws features from both general education and vocational training. It is a mixed system that uses both outcomes and competences – that is, it will deal with both capability and competence. It will emphasize basic skills and general abilities (in Australian terms, key competences) such as communication, interpersonal skills, problem solving, and adaptability.

General vocational education is concerned both with preparation for employment (and hence preparation for specific vocational training) and with encouraging educational advancement, including entry into higher education. It may be school, college or work-based. It is less subject to change than academic education and is less in need of regular updating than specific vocational training. The contribution by Hilary Steedman (see "The Issues" by Hilary Steedman in this volume) draws attention to the paradox of employers' desire for stable qualifications that respond to changing needs.

Perhaps general vocational education can offer the required element of stability. This middle path offers an open-ended option for young people who are

◆ Figure 1. **The academic/vocational continuum**

Academic Education	General Vocational Education	Specific Vocational Training
Outcomes Education-based Relatively stable	← – – – – – – → ← – – – – – – → ← – – – – – – →	Competences Employment-based Regular updating

motivated by the occupational relevance of a practical learning experience but who have not yet decided on their future direction. It provides a solid initial education foundation on which to build specific vocational training and lifelong learning. The qualifications can also be appropriate for the continuing education of adults.

Conceptualising qualifications in terms of a continuum also helps avoid associating general education with a high level, and vocational education with a low level. There will be courses/qualifications at every phase of the continuum at each of a series of levels. Moreover, some qualifications which traditionally have been thought of as academic may now be considered "general vocational", for example degrees in medicine and law.

Finally, this approach allows for diversity within a unified system. Vocational education is not required to lose its distinctive identity as the price of marriage with academic education.

3.   INTERNAL AND EXTERNAL ASSESSMENT

Consideration of the academic/vocational divide leads to reflection on another dichotomy: that between internal and external assessment. Internal assessment is that undertaken by teachers, trainers and supervisors – the people who generally know and may be responsible for the candidate's training. Internal assessment has many clear benefits for vocational education and training:

- It is more comprehensive – that is, it permits assessment of all essential outcomes instead of merely a sample.
- It encourages a focus on practical skills rather than solely the intellectual skills tested by written examinations.
- It tends to reduce instrumentality (i.e. the practice of teaching for the exam).
- It allows teachers and students to better clarify the goals of learning.
- It encourages formative assessment – that is, assessment as a part of teaching and designed to improve performance.
- It enhances teachers' professionalism.

On the other hand, there are disadvantages to internal assessment:

- It sometimes encourages fragmentation or trivialisation of the curriculum (if teachers teach and test each outcome separately).
- It changes the student/teacher relationship insofar as the teacher is judge as well as friend.
- It can create an administrative burden for teachers (if the system is too detailed and complex).

– It may lack the credibility and esteem of external assessment.

These are not fatal flaws. Steps that can be taken to deal with them include:

a) *Enhancement of teachers' skills and the feeling that they are responsible for their work:* in order to assess effectively and project a credible image for internal assessment, teachers need to be skilled in assessing and feel confident that they "own" the standards.

b) *The use of integrative assessments:* to avoid the danger of fragmentation and reduce the administrative burden, teachers need to be able to design and use assessments which cover a range of outcomes.

c) *Adoption of a mixed-mode system:* as many papers argue in this volume, it may be best to have a mixed system – that is, one employing both internal and external assessment and benefiting from the strengths of both. A mixed system will probably be necessary to unite academic and vocational education. Its adoption requires further consideration.

The issue is often posed in terms of a dichotomy between coursework that is designed and assessed internally (or by trainers in the work place) and examinations designed and marked externally. However, it is not simply a question of distinguishing between internal and external assessment but between continuous and end-of-programme assessment. While the latter tends to be external, and continuous assessment internal, this is not always the case. For example, the examinations designed and marked internally (bottom left of Figure 2) is the approach most commonly used in higher education. Who would suggest that this form of *internal assessment* lacks status?

It is also possible to have integrated projects which lie somewhere between continuous and end-of-programme assessment. Furthermore, there are various degrees of external assessment, for example tests that are designed and

◆ Figure 2. **A mixed-mode assessment system**

	INTERNAL		EXTERNAL
Continuous	Coursework and tests designed and assessed internally		Coursework and tests designed internally and assessed externally
		Standardised tests designed externally and assessed internally	
	Integrated projects		
End of course	Examinations designed and assessed internally		Examinations designed and assessed externally

standardised externally (perhaps in a national centre) and given by teachers. Conversely, coursework may be sent outside for marking.

The relationships between these modes of assessment may be understood in the form of a matrix, as set out in Figure 2.

This classification does not pretend to be exhaustive. The point is that, rather than thinking in terms of a simplistic dichotomy, we should recognise various degrees of internal and external assessment and select for each qualification a blend of approaches which best meets the goals of assessment in terms of validity, reliability, credibility and efficiency, as well as pedagogical aims such as flexibility and access. Again, we are advancing the principle of diversity in a unified system.

4.   CENTRALISATION AND DECENTRALISATION

Finally, this paper looks at institutional frameworks and organisational arrangements and subsequently the centralisation/decentralisation dilemma. VOTEC systems can benefit from using a range of different assessors, including teachers, trainers and supervisors. Some will provide training and assessment, others only assessment. This diversity is necessary to ensure a highly flexible and accessible system in which people can learn and/or be assessed not only in schools and colleges but in the work place, in the community and through distance learning.

In such a diverse and flexible system, ensuring the quality of assessment is a key issue. It is important to consider whether moderators are sufficient to safeguard the consistency of standards in teacher-based systems of assessment. Our view is that moderation is necessary but not sufficient. Other steps must be taken. First, the skills or learning standards must be clearly specified. Second, and this is very important, the standards must be internalised by VOTEC staff. This process of internalisation can be greatly assisted by publishing examples of student work which meet the required standards. This of course also helps students, employers and the general public to understand the standards.

Then comes moderation:[1] both in the sense of consensus moderation – a process by which teachers review each others' assessment and hence standardise their judgements and improve their own grasp of the standards – and external verification through a system of external checks.

The SCOTVEC (Scottish VOTEC) experience with a system based on learning outcomes and internal assessment has led to the conclusion that success is based on VOTEC staff's commitment to quality. This view concords with theories of total quality management (TQM) which currently interests many enterprises. The standards must be respected by committed and professional VOTEC staff, and responsibility for quality control should be decentralised to education and training institutions that demonstrate the capacity to undertake this. This is the path along which SCOTVEC is now leading VOTEC providers in Scotland.

However, there is a tension between, on the one hand, a decentralising trend to tap the creativity of VOTEC staff and help VOTEC institutions become mature and autonomous, and, on the other hand, a national framework of reference of learning targets and skills designed to ensure coherence and transferability. There is no easy solution to the dilemma; it is hoped that this tension is a source of creativity.

Finally, there is an issue central to the development of high-quality VOTEC, one which Scotland has yet to address. The VOTEC staff are the key resource on which quality depends. The creation of a flexible and responsive system implies the need to train or retrain work place trainers, assessors[2] and verifiers. It also suggests the need for fundamental changes to the training of teachers in schools and colleges so that they can contribute effectively to the new VOTEC systems and approaches which are emerging. It is necessary to define skills and work qualifications to reflect adequately the knowledge and skills which staff require for work in a modern VOTEC system. This may be the key that opens many doors.

NOTES

1. The expression "moderation" refers to a process sometimes also known as verification in English-speaking countries, and as harmonisation in a number of European countries. The process has as its main purpose ensuring that the assessments made by teachers conform to national standards.

2. The term "assessor" in this paper refers to those, normally teachers or trainers, who assess student performance.

COMPARABILITY AND RECOGNITION OF QUALIFICATIONS: EUROPEAN EXPERIENCES

by

Olivier Bertrand

Centre d'études et de recherches sur les qualifications, Paris

INTRODUCTION

The first section of this paper deals with the attempt at harmonising qualifications in response to the prospect of free circulation within the European Union. It focuses in turn on the cases of regulated occupations, other occupations, and students. The second section addresses the methodological problems encountered, the objectives pursued and future prospects.

The subject of qualifications immediately poses problems of definition as well as terminology, particularly when different institutional and social contexts are involved. To avoid weighing down the present text, certain remarks on the notion of qualification and related issues of terminology are treated separately in Appendix 1.

With regard to the certification of qualifications in particular, it is interesting to observe how this has been approached in the context of European Union and what difficulties have been encountered. The main question is whether, given the difference of national contexts, it is necessary or even desirable and possible to set up a single model that is common to all the member countries of the Union, or whether it would not be better simply to facilitate contacts and comparisons. This question is relevant to a variety of very different situations, including foreign study, access to certain occupations, job placement, or social and wage recognition of the qualification. The problems that arise fall into two groups: those concerning objectives (what is needed for the construction of Europe?) and those concerning methods (what is methodologically possible?).

For some time, these questions were addressed institutionally, through the search for regulations, mechanisms or tools aimed at a Community solution, whether in terms of recognition or comparability of qualifications. This approach is summarised in the first section below. Given the limitations and the methodological difficulties that emerged from this experience, however, along with questions about the goals to be attained and the real needs to be met, fresh approaches have met with greater receptivity. These approaches and their underlying problematique are analysed in the second section of this paper.

I. THE SEARCH FOR EUROPEAN HARMONISATION

The aspect of qualification that has so far drawn the most attention stems from the principle of free circulation of individuals between member countries. The application of this principle has posed three quite different kinds of problem:

- the exercise of an occupation being subject to entry regulations for citizens from another country of the Union;
- comparability of qualifications for certain occupations;
- pursuit of studies in other member countries.

Regulated occupations and the recognition of diplomas

The free circulation of workers is one of the fundamental principles of European Union, which means that legal obstacles to such circulation should be eliminated. Since the 1970s, member countries have thus barred all discrimination between citizens and foreigners from other member countries in matters of access to occupations. This has posed the problem, however, of regulated occupations, where national law restricts access to those holding a diploma (also national) or where an occupational title can only be obtained by such diploma holders. In other words, we are faced with the problem of equivalence or recognition of diplomas.

This problem had already been raised on the *bilateral level*, notably between France and Germany: Franco-German co-operation agreements have allowed for equivalencies in vocational training diplomas since 1963. In application of these agreements, delegations from the two countries undertook detailed comparisons of the content of training programmes in various fields, such as aeronautics. This particular experience illustrated some of the general difficulties encountered in such an undertaking. First of all, a detailed comparison involves considerable work and thus requires a great deal of time. As a result, few diplomas could actually be compared, and since the contents are periodically modified, some of the equivalencies were quickly outdated.

Furthermore, while it is fairly easy to identify the fields of study, it is much more difficult to compare the levels attained in each country. In fact, the two training systems are based on totally different principles. In Germany, vocational training (which normally requires at least three years) can be entered from several levels of general education, and produces heterogeneous qualifications in terms of the time required for their acquisition. In France, by contrast, vocational training enters the school system at a fixed level (the first) and requires two years of training after ten years of general education. An equivalence between the two is thus difficult to define. It is particularly debatable, moreover, when this French first level is considered the equivalent of the German dual certificate in areas where a large proportion of trainees (one-half in the case of banking) already have the *Abitur* diploma, which presupposes thirteen years of prior education.

It may be noted in passing that while the comparative analysis of training content is difficult to undertake in any systematic way in order to officially formalise equivalents among diplomas, it can be useful in comparing the operational logistics of the training systems (see, for example, the works of Hilary Steedman, in this volume and elsewhere).

On the European level, when the Brussels Commission turned to the main regulated occupations (architecture, medical professions), it was confronted not only by these technical problems but also by the interests at play in the different occupational groups. This is why a considerable amount of time was needed to reach an agreement on some twenty specific directives concerning higher degrees (sixteen years for pharmacists and eighteen for architects).

To accelerate the process, the Commission turned to the elaboration of directives leading to a general system of mutual recognition of diplomas among member countries. In 1988, at the suggestion of the Commission, the Council adopted a *first directive* concerning all post-secondary diplomas, sanctioning training programmes of at least three years after the end of secondary education. This directive, like the one that followed, represents a legal commitment on the part of member countries to seek mutual recognition of their diplomas, while retaining the right to define the modalities of application to their own context.

At present, three cases may be singled out:

– In accordance with the general principle set forth by European jurisprudence, "Every citizen of the Community has the right to require the host member country to examine and take into account the diplomas that he or she has acquired in another member country in order to determine whether they correspond to those required of its own nationals".

– Beyond this principle, recognition is automatic in the case of Community systems established by specific directives. Numbering 22 in all, these apply to different craft, manufacturing or commercial activities, doctors, nurses, pharmacists, dentists, midwives, veterinarians and architects. For these occupations, the member country retains no discretionary power over the length or content of this experience or training (since it has already recognised them).

– Recognition is termed semi-automatic in the area covered by the general directive of 1988. This concerns access to and exercise of all regulated occupations other than those already covered by a sectoral system and which require a higher education diploma corresponding to a minimum of three years' vocational training. These include notably the occupations of lawyer, accountant, engineer, psychologist and teacher. Here, the equivalence of the training programmes is assumed, although the host member country has the possibility of challenging it. The directive has been in effect since January 1991 but is not automatically applicable: each country has to modify its internal legislation accordingly. When there are substantial differences between the training programmes of two countries, the host country can request either an orientation programme or an aptitude test, but the latter cannot be an academic evaluation or follow a university model.

Situations vary from one country to another, but there are also likely to be considerable divergences in application. One significant problem that has not yet been resolved is that of civil service jobs. In principle, these are regulated occupations and thus, on the higher level at least, come under the directive. Most countries, however, still require their civil servants to be citizens. The European Court of Justice, meanwhile, holds that only posts "which participate in the exercise of public power" or "the defence of the general interests of the State" can be reserved in this way.

The problem of extending the principle of the general directive to the lower levels has presented itself for many years. One difficulty has laid in weighting the regulated occupations involved. At first glance, this seemed fairly unimportant, but on closer examination it appeared that, on the contrary, the number of these regulated occupations was much greater than at the upper level (several hundred in certain countries), with considerable differences, depending on the country. This situation helps to explain why the adoption of a second directive was a lengthy process.

This *second directive* was finally adopted on 18 June 1992. It provides for mutual recognition of diplomas obtained at the conclusion of post-secondary studies of at least one year. But it also introduces some innovations, in providing for particular systems for recognition of other qualifications which do not correspond to academic training programmes. In this way, for example, the National Vocational Qualifications which, in the United Kingdom, evaluate ability based on experience as well as on training, are accepted on an equal level with diplomas (see below). It remains to be seen how this recent directive will be implemented, since it will undoubtedly pose problems of application in member countries.

Correspondence and comparability of qualifications

The problems of equivalence evoked thus far for the regulated occupations are largely legal in nature. The situation is different for other occupations, which in fact constitute the large majority. Among the many questions that have arisen with European Union, the main one to date is the recognition of workers' qualifications in relation to their mobility from one country to another. But given that lack of information may be an obstacle to mobility, there is also the issue of better informing workers and employers, or the possible creation of a European labour market, or the alignment of policies on training preparing for different qualifications, or simply setting up a common language that can facilitate exchanges of information (statistical matters, for example).

These questions have led to the development of different EU systems or instruments. These are alternately conceived *in terms of the job or in terms of the individual qualification* (mainly for a training programme), but the distinction between the two is not always very clear. In any event, the EU has developed a *five-level grid* oriented to both an academic programme of study (*e.g.* compulsory education plus technical and vocational training) and the degree of complexity of the work to which this programme should normally lead (see definitions in Appendix 2). The grid has no legal value but should serve above all as a frame of reference, notably for the comparability of qualifications (see below). Among the problems it poses, however, is the fact that it maintains a correspondence between training and skill levels; this implicitly goes back to the hypothesis of a training-employment equivalence which has been discounted as unrealistic in all recent studies. In order to avoid an overly rigid commitment to this approach, the grid relies on extremely loose definitions; thus, at the very most it can serve as a kind of vernacular reference, with Level 2 generally assimilated to that of skilled workers.

A device that is already quite old consisted of adopting a *common vocabulary* of occupations to facilitate the exchange of employment supply and demand. SEDOC,[1] as it is called, was set up in seven languages during the 1970s. It seems to have had few applications, but it is being revised.

While SEDOC has a functional goal, the *classification of occupations* is mainly oriented toward the exchange of statistical information among specialised bodies. After the ILO adopted a new standard international classification of occupations (CITP) in 1988, the question was raised as to whether it was necessary to envision a new European classification common to the twelve member countries and distinct from that of the ILO. The comparison of existing national systems (Bertrand and Maréchal, 1992) had in fact demonstrated the impossibility of comparing national data on occupations, not only because they differ from one country to another, but even more because the structuring of the classification systems is different: one country will favour social status, another the qualification level, yet another the occupational specialisation.

After consulting the member countries, the Commission's statistics departments (EUROSTAT) decided not to develop a specific classification but to set up a transitional system allowing national data to be translated into a common classification system adaptable to that of the ILO. The Institute of Employment Research of the University of Warwick in the United Kingdom was asked to carry out this project.

Comparability of qualifications

Along with the legal question posed by access to regulated occupations, the question of access to the vast majority of other occupations has finally been raised. This is the subject of major projects on the comparability of qualifications undertaken for the Commission by the CEDEFOP[2] on the basis of a Council decision. These projects are the result of a July 1985 Council decision aimed notably at permitting the workers involved "to make better use of their qualifications, particularly in view of their access to adequate employment in another member country. The intention was to arrive at an accelerated approach common to the member countries and the Commission in order to establish the comparability of qualifications in vocational training and improve information in this area" (Sellin, 1990).

This approach "excludes formal recognition with the weight of law. But that does not keep the comparisons (...) from leading to a similar result. They could even allow workers – to the extent that there were no other national regulations on access to their occupation – to make better use of their qualifications than would have been possible with a regulation comparable to the directive on university degrees" (Sellin, 1990).

In concrete terms, these projects are carried out with the participation of representatives of all the member countries and especially the social partners. In addition to arriving at an agreement on a common definition of the main occupations, they provide the name of the corresponding occupation in each of the member countries, along with the main forms of access and the diplomas generally required.

At present, only those occupations identified with Level 2 of the European classification (skilled and clerical workers, see above) have been taken into account. In February 1992, the following occupational groups were the subject of a publication in the *Gazette of the European Communities*: hotel and restaurant management; automobile repair; construction; electricity and electronics; agriculture, horticulture and forestry; textiles and clothing; metalworking. The projects on textiles, office work, banking and insurance, commerce and chemistry were still under way.

Occupational profiles

The problems posed by comparability, which are described in greater detail in the second section of this paper, have led the CEDEFOP to explore another approach through an experimental project known as "Occupational profiles". Its orientation is different, first of all, in that the aim is transparency rather than comparability. Furthermore, the goal is not so much to set up a single system as to arrive at a better understanding of similarities and differences among the national systems. Thus, there is no attempt to define European qualifications or occupations. However, in trying to compare the national situations there is still a need for a basic frame of reference: this is no longer the occupation but all the occupational activities taken together, as defined by groups of tasks that fall within larger functions. The basic hypothesis is that these tasks and functions are practically the same everywhere, with differences between countries mainly related to the way they are broken down into occupations. It should thus be possible to define a common European grid of occupational activities which could serve as a reference for the analysis of occupations and the principal means of access to them in the twelve countries.

Such a grid would thus offer a transitional system which is, if not automatic, at least easily adaptable for different uses: comparability and recognition of qualifications, but also training. Indeed, at a second stage, the activities would be translated in terms of competences to be developed, which would provide a frame of reference for training.

Certification and pursuit of studies

The general directives just mentioned concern the recognition of vocational rather than academic diplomas. Neither the Treaty of Rome nor the Treaty on Political Union explicitly provide for the right of free circulation for students. However, the principle of non-discrimination on the basis of nationality for access to training is accepted. It is also stipulated that everyone should be able "to receive adequate training, with respect for free choice of occupation, training site, provider, and work place".

In this area, there is no general arrangement guaranteeing equivalents and automatically permitting the pursuit of studies in another European country. It has already been noted that the diversity of education systems makes comparability difficult; it must also be stressed that in their autonomy, universities usually have sole responsibility for degree criteria.

Under the circumstances, the problem of foreign study depends first of all on base-level initiatives taken by the bodies involved in order to arrive at bilateral or multilateral agreements. For its part, the Community has made certain arrangements to encourage student mobility and stimulate such initiatives. These arrangements include the following.

The Community network of national information centres on the academic recognition of higher education diplomas (NARIC), created in 1984, provides information and advice on questions of academic recognition of diplomas and periods of study undertaken in another member country. An information network on education in the Community (Eurydice) was set up in 1980 to facilitate exchanges of information on national education systems and policies. Within the framework of the Erasmus programme, the inter-university co-operation programmes (PIC) proposed by groups of institutions allow young people to pursue their education in another member country of the EU (and the EFTA since 1993), regardless of discipline or level of study.

Also within the framework of Erasmus, a pilot programme on the European Course Credit Transfer System (ECTS) has been conducted among some 145 academic institutions since 1989 to define course content in order to reach agreement on the distribution of credits for teaching units. Finally, there are various EU programmes such as Lingua, Comett and Eurotecnet intended to develop exchanges and facilitate foreign study.

2.   PROBLEMS AND PERSPECTIVES

Attempts at harmonisation or comparability raise two kinds of problems worthy of consideration: those concerning methods used and those concerning objectives pursued.

Methodological problems posed by the comparability of qualifications

The fact that projects on the comparability of qualifications and the definition of occupational profiles poses problems of more general interest warrants a closer examination of them. The Commission has just completed an assessment of projects on comparability of qualifications. The main reactions of member countries were solicited during a meeting of experts held in Nuremburg in October 1991. Apart from the time and money that such an ambitious operation requires, it raises a series of fundamental questions, two of which can be cited here.

First, given that comparability will, in the first stage, apply only to European Level 2 qualifications, *what are the criteria* for determining the level of occupational activity?[3]

The European classification indicates that this level "corresponds to a complete qualification for a precise activity, accompanied by a mastery of the instruments and techniques necessary for the exercise of this activity. The means of access to this level is normally the required education followed by technical or vocational training". As may have been noted, this definition provides an excellent illustration of "the ambiguity of the terminology used...". Are they speaking about comparability of diplomas or about in-house qualifications linked to the jobs held? The different countries do not have the same conceptual references. In the case of Germany, for example, "the same social partners negotiate job content, training content, standards for diplomas and the positioning of the job in the classification grid" (Pasquier, 1989). This is quite different from the French case, characterised by diverse sites and goals of negotiations. The identification of a "skilled operative" level is particularly difficult, in view of present changes in the work world, as a result of which the kind of competences required depends less on easily identified tradi-

tional know-how and more on personal qualities (such as responsibility or autonomy) that are difficult to situate on a grid.

A second objection concerns the *difficulty of reaching a consensus* among
representatives of the twelve countries on a common definition of a "qualification".
Here the problem faced is that of comparability among different kinds of work
organisation, but even more so among several systems of training, occupational
classification and, more broadly, social relations. In other words, this is the "societal effect" that was the subject of classic studies by Maurice, Sellier and Sylvestre
(1982) in France and by Lutz in Germany. In order to overcome this difficulty, there
is great risk of reaching a consensus based on the lowest common denominator – in
other words, a restrictive, imprecise and ultimately not very meaningful definition.
Such definitions would correspond neither to a "European" situation, which is only
an abstract concept, nor to any national reality.

The approach aimed at the *definition of occupational profiles* responds in large
part to the objections raised over the comparability of qualifications. Nonetheless,
it presents serious difficulties, as listed below.

Developing a frame of reference for occupational activities already constitutes
a considerable investment on the national level. On the European level, such an
investment must be even greater if its validity is to be guaranteed. One problem is
the degree of detail incorporated into the description. A detailed analysis runs the
risk of being cumbersome, too specific to one country or one particular context, and
quickly outdated. Conversely, a description that is too broad (based, for example,
on large functions) would probably be vague and open to different interpretations
by each country.

Even if a common frame of reference were developed, the comparison with
national occupational definitions calls into question the existence and validity of
the latter. In this respect, three kinds of situation present themselves in Europe. In
certain countries there is one, and only one, generally recognised national system
for classifying and defining occupations. This is the most favourable situation but it
is not very frequent. In the second case, there is no system of this kind, and the
question is who will define the occupations and what will be the value and degree
of recognition of these definitions? Here it must be stressed that given the infinite
diversity of work situations, no expert can easily propose appropriate and generally
acceptable definitions; thus, significant investigation and consultation are
necessary.

Finally, there is a third situation, marked not by one but by several systems of
occupational classification and definition. This is the case in France, where a
statistical classification, a job directory, an occupational directory for placement,
occupational classifications and information for student guidance all co-exist. Since
each of these instruments has its own justification, it is difficult to say what *the*
definition of an occupation is. Indeed, the very concept of occupation has various

dimensions (specialisation, function, nature and degree of difficulty, remuneration, social status and position as self-employed or employee). One dimension or another will be emphasized according to its uses (statistical analysis, placement, orientation, training). The identification of occupations is thus far from an elementary technical task following simple rules.

Situating themselves more in the context of training than that of occupational mobility, projects on occupational profiles seek to arrive at the *analysis of competences* necessary for the exercise of a work activity and thus at the identification and possibly comparison of training needs. This approach poses the problem of the very idea of competence and the possibility of defining it in a way that is clear, generally accepted and functional. In the United Kingdom it is this idea that informs the major project under way to define the National Vocational Qualifications, which are intended to develop a clear, common standard that will help to orient training toward the satisfaction of economic needs (Rencontre d'experts, 1991). The competences thus defined should have a national value, and it is hoped that the method, if not the results, will be transferable on the European level. The French Directory of Occupations and Jobs (Répertoire opérationnel des métiers et des emplois: ROME) is based on entirely different goals and methodology: it also provides brief definitions of the competences and capacities necessary for a work activity, but with reference to a specific occupation and in the context of job placement rather than training.

A different conception has been put forward by Gabriel Fragnière earlier in this volume, for whom "competences are composed by the individual and ultimately subjective ability to use one's qualifications, know-how and knowledge to accomplish something. In fact, there are no objective competences capable of being defined independently of the individuals in which they are embodied. There are no competences in and of themselves; there are only competent people. This has a direct influence on the recognition of these competences and their transferability (...). Competences cannot be measured independently of the individuals who possess them (...). Whereas knowledge and qualifications are the result of a training activity or a course of study, competences are always the outcome of experience". According to this conception, therefore, competences cannot come under a generalised frame of reference.

Even if such conceptual difficulties were to be surmounted, on a more functional level the identification of competences is still likely to meet several pitfalls. On the one hand, in the interests of objectivity, there is an attempt to define the tasks or activities carried out; this comes back to much the same process as that of the occupational profiles, and entails the same problems. On the other hand, these tasks and activities are translated in terms of knowledge, know-how and behaviours, which then poses a problem of interpretation. On the psychological level, it is far from clear what is really necessary for carrying out a work activity, given the role of the context (state of the labour market at a given time and place) and the characteristics of the individual, not to mention the analytical sensitivity required. This difficulty looms particularly large for what have been called the three-dimensional competences, and these are precisely the ones that most interest companies today insofar as they involve behaviours: problem-solving ability and power of expression, but also motivation, firm loyalty, etc. These factors are quite subjective and conditioned by the environment. Where then should the list stop? Who can determine the relative importance of each factor?

The project of the National Vocational Qualifications in the United Kingdom addresses these difficulties by making the operation a national priority with considerable means allocated to it. Such an effort certainly encourages a degree of *de facto* consensus about its results, but there is still room for question about the validity of defining a methodology that is widely accepted because it is scientifically based.

There is all the more reason to think that on the European level, the use of a competence-based approach will present even greater problems. In addition to national specifications involving forms of organisation and division of labour, work relations and educational systems, there are also cultural differences. Given these variations – in the role of general culture, the degree of specialisation, the status of the manual worker or the engineer – it appears questionable whether the notion of competence can be defined and interpreted in the same way from one country to another, since it is already quite difficult to do so from one individual or work situation to another.

This critical analysis should not be taken to deny the value of comparing approaches, or seeking points of convergence, or conducting comparative studies on a particular activity sector or occupational group, based on a common methodology. The approach underlying the project on occupational profiles could provide a base for this kind of work; however, it is not clear how this could generate a directory-type document that would be functional and easily consulted by a large public.

3. WHICH GOALS? WHICH NEEDS?

Freedom of access to regulated occupations necessarily depends on a Community approach. In this respect, real enforcement of the directives is still an objective, notably in the case of civil service jobs, and this is a problem of a legal and political nature. With regard to the other qualifications, however, given the methodological difficulties ones posed by the harmonisation or development of instruments of comparability, there are still questions to be raised about the precise objectives implied by the construction of Europe and the needs that it should meet.

The projects aimed at elaborating systems of recognition, correspondence or comparability have been based primarily on the *hypothesis of a development of occupational mobility* among the countries of the EU. This hypothesis does not seem to be confirmed, however, either by the statistics on recent trends or by more qualitative investigations conducted in firms. Quantitatively, the main source of mobility to date has been the disequilibrium between the poorest countries, where the unemployment rate was high, and those that offered greater opportunities. Within the EU, such disequilibrium is in fact tending to disappear. Apart from managerial positions, geographical mobility is very weak even within individual European countries, and this is even more true when it entails crossing borders and confronting difficulties of an institutional, cultural and, above all, linguistic order.

At present, and in the short term, we can say that geographical mobility among countries of the EU involves mainly frontier workers, managers and students. In most cases, the qualification of frontier workers is fairly low, and the problem of recognition hardly presents itself. The same is true when there is a strong demand for labour power, which makes employers less concerned with qualification (*cf.* the case of Luxembourg). What is important is the level of remuneration, which depends on the labour market conditions, and notably the employer's assessment of the worker's competence and efficiency rather than any formal evaluation. This is also the case for those few occupations in which mobility is traditionally strong, such as hotel and restaurant management: foreign workers are judged much more in relation to their past experience and concrete demonstration of know-how than on the basis of their diplomas.

In particular fields, and especially among certain large multinationals, the international mobility of managers is virtually becoming a condition for professional advancement among young people. Some multinationals have undertaken studies on the value of foreign degrees, although the majority consider that they already have sufficient information, since they can draw, by definition, on a network of contacts who will supply them with information on institutions in the countries where they operate. In any case, if the problem does arise, it is only at the time of initial recruitment, generally at the beginning of an individual's career. And in fact, it is even less frequent since, when international mobility is an integral part of a professional career, the managers involved remain connected to their original firm with the corresponding status. At least, this is the point of view of the companies; that of the workers may be different, when they feel themselves unjustly ranked in the company classification system. There is at least one case of a French engineer employed in Germany who was not ranked at the same level as his German counterparts because the organisation of instruction in his school was not the same as that of other French engineering schools. It is difficult, however, to say to what extent this was an isolated case.

Student mobility, meanwhile, can be seen as a goal in itself (to advance European union through the intermixing of its youth population), but also as a precondition of occupational mobility (studying in several countries would help to surmount psychological and practical obstacles, if only on the linguistic level). This student mobility does in fact appear to be growing, and there is a demand that is not always met. It is still very difficult for a young person raised in more than one country and mastering several languages to pursue higher education abroad and acquire truly international training, insofar as the recognition of degrees or credits is not automatic, and the consistency of the programmes far from guaranteed. Thus, there is a need for harmonisation or co-ordination among European countries, and after free access to regulated occupations, this can be considered a second essential goal for European policy making.

This somewhat sceptical assessment of mobility should perhaps be qualified in a long-term perspective. There is, for example, the possibility of new forms of mobility linked to the development of international employment pools, the extension of exchanges within extra-national geographical entities, and the creation of R&D centres in response to the spread of technological innovations (Merle, 1992). In this instance, the question bears more particularly on the recognition of intermediate qualifications (highly skilled operatives and clerical employees and especially technicians). This is the group that faces the fewest problems in terms of recognition of qualifications, since it is less mobile than the categories at the two extremes. But should its mobility increase, it is at this level that the most problems would arise since it is the least well identified, the most subject to change and the most sensitive to national specifications, from the point of view of jobs and training programmes alike.

A third type of goal might involve comparative studies on, for example, the organisation of labour, the definition of occupations, the conditions for access to jobs, conditions of employment, occupational classifications and conditions for recognition of qualification, or training structures and programmes. This kind of project would require a scientific approach in order to resolve the difficult problems of comparability. It represents a considerable investment and can only be carried out by specialised teams. Such a project should therefore be focused on a well-defined field: an economic activity sector or a group of occupations or training programmes. The field selected would normally correspond to areas in which particular problems arise, either where mobility is stronger, where a change in qualifications is observed or anticipated, or where there is a desire to pose the problem of training on the European level. But the fragmentary nature of this project does not contradict the desire to harmonise methodologies and capitalise on research. It is in this way that progress can gradually be made toward a common language and a shared approach.

Finally, it is obvious that there is a need for information and exchange on the foreign systems. This seems to be the case primarily with regard to the understanding of training systems, not simply in terms of a description but, above all, the operational logic proper to each system. In Germany, for example, this would cover the relations between general and vocational training or the variable length of higher education programmes. Information on employment systems is also needed: what are the different kinds of work contracts or occupational classifications, what are company recruitment practices, etc?

In this area of information, it is clear once again that there is no single system meeting the diverse needs of the various users: those of workers are necessarily different from those of employers, employers' organisations, or training or placement institutions. Simple and rapidly accessible information systems for the most concrete elements must co-exist with more technical files for the analysis and comparison of complex systems. A whole series of projects and mechanisms are being developed by EU bodies. Their effectiveness will depend on the effort of synthesis and readability devoted to them and on their adaptation to this diversity of needs.

The spread of information is not limited to the production of documents, however: direct exchanges among partners are just as important. In this respect, it may be noted that all the participants in the CEDEFOP projects on the comparability of qualifications have indicated that what benefited them most was the opportunity to meet their counterparts from other countries and in this way get to know and understand different systems of training and employment. Likewise, the discussions arising from projects on degree equivalencies for access to regulated occupations "constitute an important point of reference within each country for the definition of these occupations (...). Given the major changes in academic programmes and conditions of granting degrees just about everywhere in Europe (...) the European dialogue in this area cannot help but have an impact on the national debates" (Merle, 1992). In any event, the continuation and, if possible, intensification of this kind of exchange is to be desired.

Finding an institutional solution for access to regulated occupations, facilitating student mobility, carrying out comparative studies and distributing suitable information: these seem to be the key responses to the problems posed thus far in the area of qualification on the European level. This outlook differs from the initial approach which, with its orientation towards directories and complex standardised mechanisms, was more instrumental. It must be recognised, however, that there is still a demand for the latter, notably in countries that do not yet have national standards and are hoping that such structures will provide the framework they are lacking. This is also true for certain union leaders who, fearing the social consequences of the opening of the borders, feel that European standards could prevent a degree of labour market deregulation. Weighed against the methodological difficulties summarised above and the analysis of needs to be met, however, these arguments do not seem to be sufficiently convincing to justify mechanisms that offer the further inconvenience of a very high cost and the risk of rapid obsolescence.

In any case, the recognition of qualification does not impose itself unilaterally: it results from the concrete operating conditions of each labour market. It is not because an official document cites a given degree or occupation that employers will necessarily take this into account in evaluating the workers they recruit. At the very most, it can provide an argument or a point of reference in negotiations between employers and unions. The problem already presents itself in these terms within most European countries and will inevitably be taken up during this seminar. The same is inevitably the case and, all the more so, for comparisons among qualifications of different countries.

4.   NEW QUESTIONS, NEW APPROACHES

Most recently, the Brussels Commission, along with the opinions of experts that it has generated, has moved towards a broader approach to the problems of qualification.

Recognition of acquired experience

There is now general agreement, in principle at least, on the fact that qualifications cannot be evaluated solely in terms of a diploma, and even less a single initial training diploma. The necessity of adapting to accelerated changes in jobs and the development of continuing training (which most often does not lead to a diploma) have contributed to this new awareness. One of the advantages of the British National Vocational Qualifications approach is to establish the principle that such qualifications can be recognised in a variety of forms, with considerable importance being attached to work experience. For several years, this awareness has also been apparent in France, where it has given rise to a series of new orientations and projects (Colardyn, 1990). In Germany, meanwhile, the very principle of the dual system guarantees that vocational as well as academic experience is taken into account and provides for graded steps recognised by a diploma.

On the EU level, the problem is increasingly cited in the current debates within member countries as well as in consultants' studies and reports. The latter stress the necessity of not limiting systems of certification to a purely academic rationale but, rather, opening them up to work experience and placing the two structures in mutual contact. The EU's role should be that of facilitating this overture. "The point is not to implement, on the supra-national level, a new formality for certification but to utilise the Community dimension of the market to induce change in the overly static and formal structures often existing in the member countries" (Fragnière, 1992).

One of the approaches envisioned for the recognition of acquired experience is the progressive implementation of a system based on the "portfolio of competences" (a term coined in the United States). What this entails is simply the normalisation of a worker's successive experiences presented in the form of a file that he or she is responsible for maintaining. It is thus an open-ended system which the social partners stress has nothing to do with the old "worker's booklet" that was more like a means of police control. Here, the portfolio of competences falls within a rationale of *transparency* rather than *standardisation* of certification.

It is clear that the approach based on recognition of acquired experiences is at once richer and more flexible than the other approaches examined so far. To the extent that it focuses on the singularity of the individual and his or her itinerary, however, it does not offer the same possibilities of relative positioning. It would thus be difficult to use this approach as a standard or a classification tool, whether for collective conventions, planning, or general work force management.

It would be interesting to compare the experience of European countries with that of immigrant societies (like that of Quebec) which are already receptive to the fact that the work force has acquired its qualifications in other systems. But the complexity of the European problem could not be overlooked, given the relationships that have to be worked out between training, classification, status and remuneration.

Exchanges, co-operation and the European social dialogue

Quite apart from national or university diplomas, it must be pointed out that the problem of recognition also concerns various training organisations preparing for other diplomas. This is the case, for example, with the Chambers of Commerce and bodies such as the Association for the Vocational Training of Adults (AFPA) in France. These organisations meet together to arrive at bilateral or multilateral agreements of mutual recognition or to finalise common training programmes.

If, as already observed, the heterogeneity of training systems considerably complicates comparisons and thus the attempts to define equivalents, it would appear to be less difficult to collaborate on developing new training programmes. In fact, this idea has inspired several EU programmes (COMETT, Erasmus). Here, the development of common training instruction and modules falls within a rationale of problem-sharing and complementary initiatives to permit the improvement of the quality of the training offered through the exchange of information. Likewise, the PETRA programme's network of training partnerships has led to joint training activities for trainers of youth populations. Possibilities of creating common training units are also being developed (Human Resources Task Force, 1992b). This idea has inspired a private initiative as well: the "New skills" project undertaken by a number of training organisations, including the AFPA cited above. With the support of the EU, this project is being tested in areas of joint interest to the member countries.

A European market for qualifications?

The emergence of a European market for qualifications is often evoked today by EU bodies, but its content remains largely open. In any event, it should be clear that recognition, harmonisation or comparability of qualifications must not be an end in itself. In this area, the main objective of the building of Europe should be that of raising the level and development of qualifications in the different member countries, with the dual aims of improving economic competitiveness on the one hand and promoting social cohesiveness and possibilities for workers' development on the other. To these ends, every opportunity for encounter or exchange can become a source of progress.

Within such a perspective, it seems clear that the Europe of qualifications will not necessarily come about through geographical mobility. Nor is it limited to the formal recognition of initial training. In view of the new demographic situation which is curtailing the renewal of the work force, what is required above all is an effort to improve and adapt the qualification of active workers. This is a question not only of developing the training supply but also of motivating employers to adopt work force management practices that will encourage the qualification, training and vocational advancement of their personnel. Indeed, "the firms are not only 'consumers' of qualifications produced elsewhere but also sites for the production of knowledge, know-how and development of learning situations" (Merle, 1992). The European social dialogue, undertaken in a concrete fashion on the level of the economic activity sectors, can contribute to general progress in these areas, taking into account the various problems posed by qualification and recognition.

NOTES

1. *Système européen de diffusion des offres et des demandes d'emploi enregistrées en compensation internationale* (European system of distribution of supply and demand of employment recorded in international compensation).

2. *Centre européen pour le développement de la formation professionnelle* (European centre for the development of vocational training), the Berlin-based EU organisation responsible for problems of vocational training.

3. The same problem obviously turns up in the national occupational classifications determining remunerations. Whatever the criteria used, it is ultimately the object of a negotiation between social partners rather than the result of an objective analysis. The methods of job evaluation used by firms lay claim to defining objective criteria, but everything depends on the experts who interpret them and the particular social context that makes this interpretation largely acceptable to those involved. Finally, national mechanisms for the analysis of jobs and competences also run into the problem of the level. The French Job Directory has given up on reporting it altogether; this is not the case for the National Vocational Qualifications, but these define an internal hierarchy of competences rather than jobs.

QUALIFICATION: CONCEPTS AND TERMINOLOGY

The term *qualification* is particularly ambiguous, in the language in general and in the French context in particular. In France, distinctions have often been made between the qualification of the individual (tied mainly to training and experience) and that of the work station (mainly concerning specific know-how and behaviours), and the wage category resulting from a compromise between the two in a given situation of social relations which has led to stressing that qualification was in fact a social issue bridging the world of training and that of production. Since this question is addressed here in the context of Europe and an international meeting held in several languages, it is important to clarify at the very outset the concepts and terminology, in French and English, namely:

– **Educational qualifications** (in French, *diplôme*) formalise experiences, most often of an academic nature, in an institutional system determined by the national context.

– **Training,** in the broad sense *(formation*, also in the broad sense), can be acquired in a variety of situations and can be analysed by level (expressed in numbers of years) or by a detailed examination of the subjects studied.

– The **job** *(situation de travail particulière)*, in a regular and socially identifiable form, may be called an *occupation (profession)*. The term may refer to *job contents (la nature du travail effectué)* but also to social status, remuneration or working conditions.

– **Competence** *(compétence)* is more difficult to define and will be addressed in greater detail below. For the moment, the term could refer to the individual's capacity to carry out an occupational activity in a concrete work situation, drawing on an ensemble of skills *(capacités)* which can entail specific knowledge, know-how and behaviours. Competence is an overall characteristic: it can be compared to a wall, with each skill constituting one of the bricks (Jallade, 1988).

– **Job classification** *(classification professionnelle)* takes into account all of the previous elements to situate the worker or the activity in the world of work and, in particular, to determine its remuneration.

- Finally, the term **qualification** can also refer to the whole of a worker's acquired experience, encompassing initial and continuing training along with the different stages of his or her work experience.

The necessity of evoking these different elements stems from the fact that they are so interrelated that it is not always easy to distinguish them. Moreover, situations differ considerably among the European countries. Suffice it to recall the distinction between systems based on apprenticeship and those that are mainly academic, or that between centralised and decentralised structures. The diversity is even greater in the case of the relationship between the training and labour markets. Contrasts could, for example, be drawn between:

- The French usage, which distinguishes between the granting of diplomas and the wage classification. While the former is a State monopoly based primarily on the level of studies, the latter – defined by an agreement among the social partners or by the concrete conditions of the labour market – does not necessarily take the diploma into account and is applied at the discretion of the firms.

- The German approach where, on the contrary, recognised occupations and vocational training diplomas are identical. Since firms have primary responsibility for this training, its recognition on the labour market is not at issue, nor is there the diversity of interpretations of the term *qualification* that is found in France.

- The British tendencies aimed at remedying the deficiencies of apprenticeship and the dispersion of non-recognised technical training programmes on the labour market through groups of vocational qualifications mainly defined and evaluated by employers in order to orient training towards a vocational end.

- Last of all, the situation of other countries that do not have a national system for the definition of qualification, which leaves each firm great latitude to classify its personnel.

Appendix 2

EUROPEAN CLASSIFICATION OF TRAINING LEVELS

The Structure of Training Levels in the European Union

Level 1   Training providing access to this level: compulsory education and professional initiation. This professional initiation is acquired at an educational establishment outside of the school-based training programme or through sandwich training. The volume of theoretical knowledge and practical capabilities involved is very limited. This form of training must primarily enable the holder to perform relatively simple work and may be fairly quickly acquired.

Level 2   Training providing access to this level: compulsory education and vocational training (including, in particular, apprenticeships). This level corresponds to one where the holder is fully qualified to engage in a specific activity with the capacity to use the instruments and techniques relating thereto. This activity involves chiefly the performance of work which may be independent within the limits of the relevant techniques.

Level 3   Training providing access to this level: compulsory education and/or vocational training and additional technical training or technical educational training or other secondary-level training. This form of training involves a greater fund of theoretical knowledge than that at Level 2. Activity involves chiefly technical work which can be performed independently and/or entail executive and co-ordination duties.

Level 4   Training providing access to this level: secondary training (general or vocational) and post-secondary technical training. This form of training involves high-level technical training acquired at or outside educational establishments. The resultant qualification covers a higher level of knowledge and of capabilities. It does not generally require mastery of the scientific bases of the various areas concerned. Such capabilities and knowledge make it possible in a generally autonomous or independent way to assume design and/or management and/or administrative responsibilities.

Level 5   Training providing access to this level: secondary training (general or vocational) and complete higher training. This form of training generally leads to an autonomously pursued vocational activity – as an employer or as a self-employed person – entailing a mastery of the scientific bases of the occupation.

THE ISSUE OF CERTIFICATION
THE CASE OF PORTUGAL EXPERIENCE AND
THE EUROPEAN DIMENSION

by

Luis Imaginario
Consultant, Quaternaire Ressources Humaines, Lisbon
Faculty of Psychology and Educational Sciences, University of Porto

INTRODUCTION

The value of diplomas or certificates issued by educational institutions depends on the recognition extended to them by society and the labour market. In Portugal, the problem of certification has become particularly acute over the last half dozen years. As European Community assistance became available, there was an unprecedented upsurge in the training market. The expansion was so sudden that no organised response – preparing facilities, materials and trainers – could be made.

Programmes proliferated, both at experienced institutions and at others ill-equipped to provide training. Unregulated sources of training sprang up. The country had no reliable, established system for producing qualifications and occupational skills which could set standards for this diverse supply of training, in itself a healthy development. The result was occasional misuse of funds and a certain amount of poor training.

Great efforts were made to regulate access to financial assistance for vocational training, however, and the funds are now being properly allocated. The training market has become somewhat clearer, which has improved quality – but only by winnowing out "pseudo-supply" and the most flagrant cases of unfair competition through administrative sanctions. A systematic effort is still required to promote quality programmes, largely on the technical and pedagogical side (training profiles, adaptation of training content to qualification objectives, learning processes).

It was recognised that certification, which had at first been intended for training designed to impart occupational qualifications and skills, could also decisively improve quality, which it would authenticate. The training market would remain entirely free, but it would become possible, through appropriate certification mechanisms, to separate the wheat from the chaff (*i.e.* separate those kinds of training that successfully imparted occupational qualifications and skills from those that failed to do so) and to foster competition between training programmes that clearly did impart such qualifications.

Training certification should give a better idea not only of the market but also of the demand for training programmes and qualified personnel. Prospective trainees have to base their choice of programme on the expected results, while employers have to choose between training certificates that may or may not represent the same qualifications. Both need a range of information in order to evaluate and compare the alternatives and choose wisely. Appropriate certification mechanisms would make their decisions easier: they could motivate people to invest in certified training and encourage the hiring of holders of certified qualifications.

Training supply had been bound to increase in number and variety from the mid-1970s on, with the democratisation of Portuguese society, quite apart from Community assistance which reinforced the trend. The question of certification as an instrument for clarifying and regulating the training market would have arisen sooner or later in any case; joining the European Community simply made it more urgent. Emigration − which long predated Portugal's accession to the Community − also had an impact.

I. THE EUROPEAN DIMENSION

As the deadline approached for free movement of workers in 1993, European Union directives had to be introduced (see Olivier Bertrand earlier in this volume). Portugal took part in discussions on the two directives that were adopted, and transposed the first into national law. In Portugal these directives, perhaps not models of conceptual clarity, raised expectations out of all proportion to their objectives and scope, since their only purpose is to remove obstacles to access to regulated occupations. Recognition procedures therefore apply only to them.

European Union directives have virtually nothing specific or of great importance to say about certification. The only distinction they make − not always clearly, given the large number of rules and exceptions − is between "diplomas", "certificates" and "skills certificates". It can hardly be said their intent is to foster progress in specifically regulated occupations, of which there are few in most EU countries. In Portugal, however, there is a widespread impression that the best safeguard for emigrants' qualifications − and also those of Portuguese nationals *vis-à-vis* emigrants from other member countries coming to work in Portugal − would be to provide Portuguese workers with "vocational certificates", which would entitle them to work at certain jobs − it was thought that the European Union was encouraging this approach.

2. SKILL CERTIFICATION AND REGULATION OF THE EXERCISE OF A PROFESSION

Putting aside the subtleties of interpreting the directives, our main concern here is that matters that used to be clear are clear no longer. Previously, the term "certification" was used for training which led to occupational qualifications and skills. Therefore, even when "occupational certification" was spoken of, that clearly meant "certification of occupational qualifications".

More recently, while "occupational certification" is used with that meaning, it may also be synonymous with regulation of an occupation. The distinction is important, for the first case involves regulation of training, and the second case regulation of occupations.

The evident skewing of the meaning of the European Union directives raises a very pertinent concern: how are qualifications to be acquired by those who have learned their skills not through training but on the job? This situation is common to a large part of the Portuguese labour force. Certification should primarily relate to qualifications obtained through systematic initial training, but also to qualifications acquired through experience, through the exercise of an occupation involving informal learning, possibly supplemented by short-term training courses.

All that is a far cry from the regulation of an occupation, which should be completely separate from certification, for a number of reasons. First, although qualification is often one aspect of the regulation of an occupation, it is usually only one of many conditions, the rest of which may be of a very different nature. Next, occupational regulation should be limited to such areas as health and safety, and should never seek to regulate supply and demand of qualified labour (a very different matter from regulation of the supply and demand of qualifying training); that would be tantamount to an administrative limit on the right to work, and unconstitutional in Portugal. Lastly, it is our belief that consensus may be achieved between divergent interests when it comes to generating qualifications through training; regulation of occupations, however, is apt to generate conflicts, and interests are more difficult to reconcile in this area.

Two further aspects should be considered. The distinction between the two areas does not mean that they do not interact: regulation of the supply of training should normally result in regulation of the market for skilled workers, but that comes about through the operation of market forces, not by administrative fiat. In addition, trying to regulate an occupation generally and to make it subject to certified training would very likely result in a proliferation of schools churning out certificates which would eventually prove valueless.

3. THE PROBLEM OF QUALIFICATION LEVELS

Any solution based on certification of qualifications will come up against one great difficulty, however. Reference to qualification immediately brings to mind the five levels of qualification defined by the European Community in 1985 (Portugal has had the equivalent since 1973). Clearly, there is not necessarily a one-to-one correspondence between any given occupational training or experience and one of these five levels. Some training or experience, because it falls between the cracks of this grid, will be uncertifiable.

The five levels, though useful, are only an abstraction. They correlate responsibility and autonomy and so may be understood as "levels of qualification" in the narrow sense, but they also reflect certain levels and characteristics of training that must, instead, be looked at from the point of view of "levels of training" (on this point too, see Olivier Bertrand earlier). The solution whereby only qualifications corresponding to one of the five levels would be certified cannot be rejected out of hand. Several arguments could be advanced in its favour: it would give credibility to certification, which would be conferred only on training that produced a given level of qualification; it would stimulate restructuring of training, whether initial, continuing or supplementary, and its reorientation towards certification. That would not restrict free supply of training, but would only oblige it to respect certain criteria in producing occupational qualifications.

There appears to be no reason, however, to reduce the concept of qualification to the five European levels. Any training, like any experience, can be said to produce some qualification in the broad sense of a set of occupational skills, attitudes and behaviours. It should be possible to place these somewhere in the classification, at one of the five levels or in between.

Another solution, then, would be to introduce intermediate levels, 2(a) between levels 2 and 3 for instance, and so on. That would be consistent with the changing character of the five-level classification, which is generally recognised to have rather blurred demarcations. One disadvantage: it could make the process of certification overly complex.

A third solution, which might supplement the first, would be to create, in addition to the occupational qualification certificate, one or more other kinds of credentials covering qualifications (or experience) not assignable to any of the five levels. This would accommodate the diversity of training and the many ways and means used to acquire it. It would have at least two disadvantages, however. What terminology should be used in the credentials? What hierarchical relationships would there be between types of certificate, to match qualification levels, and how would they be established?

It would be to best to certify only qualifications matching one of the five levels and to institutionalise one type of occupational "qualification" certificate. (Outside this system, training not leading to an occupational qualification would continue to be offered and would confer such diplomas as were deemed appropriate, but not the recognised occupational certificate.) The certificate would state how the qualification was obtained (training, experience or a combination of the two), the occupational profile and, where appropriate, the training profile and qualification level.

4. RECENT LEGISLATION IN PORTUGAL

Portugal has been preparing legislation on these lines. To some extent, it is patterned after the third solution mentioned above, with an occupational training certificate and an occupational aptitude certificate. The first certifies that its holder has achieved the objectives set out in the training curriculum and *a)* has reached a given qualification level, *b)* has received a grounding in the occupation in question, and *c)* has received the equivalent of a school education. The occupational aptitude certificate is an official document certifying: *a)* proficiency in the occupation in question, attested by training certificates, experience or documents issued in other countries, particularly member States of the European Union, *b)* a qualification level, *c)* the equivalent of a school education, where appropriate, and *d)* the fulfilment of such other conditions as may be required for the occupation. Both flow from the concept of occupational certification: "By occupational certification is meant the confirmation of occupational training, experience or qualifications and, where appropriate, the fulfilment of such other conditions as may be required for the occupation".

We accept that this approach may have the disadvantages mentioned earlier. The concept of occupational certification on which the system is based appears ambiguous, since it includes virtually everything – training, experience, qualifications, and other conditions – and hence lacks any rigorous operational content, with the danger of certifying little or nothing. The use of the term "aptitude", on which there is no consensus, even in psychology, seems unfortunate; it may perpetuate a number of misapprehensions. Lastly, having two kinds of certificate necessarily creates a ranking and therefore a danger that the training certificate will carry less weight than the aptitude certificate, which represents the "real" occupational certification.

Three further comments can be made. First, the devaluation of training certificates results from a concern to recognise and in some way legitimise every training course or process, something we do not find either necessary or useful. It will not lead to better training programmes and there is a danger that low-quality training will proliferate. Second, the idea behind having two types of certificate was that qualifications could be achieved either through training or through experience. But there seems no absolute need for two certificates: as suggested, one would suffice if it recognised several qualification paths without explicitly or implicitly devaluing any of them (the risk with two kinds of certificate). Finally, the terminology used for the two certificates may give the mistaken idea that the purpose of the training certificate is to regulate the training market, while the aptitude certificate is meant to regulate the occupation.

Must these disadvantages be accepted? Why has this system been instituted? There are many possible answers. First, because of the upsurge in training supply, the diversity of providers, and free worker movement, certification has become an acute problem. Second, the fact that a large part of the work force has acquired qualifications through experience has brought the government under pressure from employers and unions. Last, giving legitimacy to on-the-job vocational training, alongside the training dispensed through the educational system, has probably been a priority. The latter, though it does not yet have an occupational certification system, carries institutional prestige as part of the educational system.

Tellingly, both certificates call for the equivalent of a school education. This seems to be the wrong way to frame the problem, since we consider that, to produce vocational qualifications and skills, training must in any case include an academic component ("academic empowerment"), which is often likened to an education in the general programme and is no doubt a necessary part of any real qualification.

Another criticism of the system of on-the-job occupational certification now being developed relates to its co-ordination. Though the principle of tripartite co-ordination between government, business and workers is not debatable, the way it is implemented certainly is. The fact that co-ordination is centred in the Institute of Employment and Vocational Training, which also co-ordinates the training system and determines its financing and curriculum, may compromise its independence in evaluating, certifying and recognising the products of the system. The representation and footing of the various parties involved also raise problems. Lastly, more careful distinctions should be made between functions: ongoing or temporary technical activities, drafting of legislation, day-to-day management, and policy formulation.

In our view, the grey areas arise from a lingering uncertainty, already highlighted in this paper, as to the purpose and objective of certification. Is the aim to produce qualifications and vocational skills, mainly through training and occasionally through experience, or to use these qualifications on the labour market? In other words, is the purpose to prepare for an activity or to exercise it? Is the objective to regulate production of and access to qualifications, especially through training but also through experience, or to regulate the particular occupation? The two sets of questions are interrelated, but the first set should take precedence. The main purpose of certification must be to produce occupational qualifications and skills, and its objective be to regulate that process so as to meet the needs of a given occupation, without seeking to regulate occupations generally, save in exceptional cases where the consumers of certain goods and the users of certain services need to be protected.

5. OUTLINE OF A CERTIFICATION SYSTEM

If the problem is posed in these terms, the way to address it is to institutionalise a certification system closely linked to the training system, whose – desirable – diversity is another question. The certification system thus comprises different qualification levels and several training areas corresponding to the various types of occupational activity. The linkage does not mean that any and all training has to be certified (it may have objectives other than occupational qualification), only that those kinds of training that do seek to produce skills and qualifications must meet a given set of requirements. As already indicated, there is no reason why a given type of training, not *a priori* intended to meet such requirements, should not be certified *a posteriori*, in recognition of its mode of delivery or a restructuring of training supply.

Such a certification system, like the one planned for Portugal, will have three constituencies: trainers, employers and current holders of the qualification. The first consists of training institutes and trainers' representatives. Employers include business representatives, but also consumers, as users. Those who already hold a qualification will be represented by trade unions. There could also be some representation of trainee candidates, their families, and target groups that do not yet have access to training. Such diversity should not mask two essential points: that the three pillars of the system are training institutes, employers' associations and trade unions, and that co-ordination of the system should be the responsibility of training institutes in general, not vested in any one institute.

Co-ordination should have high institutional priority, without becoming a cumbersome apparatus. It should have very competent personnel who can assemble, analyse and disseminate information on occupations and training. Their task would be to define, update and evaluate training profiles that can be certified and will therefore correspond in a flexible way to occupational profiles. Setting requirements for certification will make it possible to develop principles governing the establishment of alternative training pathways leading to qualifications at the same level, to recognise equivalent and corresponding credentials for further training, and to lay down a credit system for partial training and occupational experience. This last point will be essential in linking initial and continuing training with a view to retraining, conversion or specialisation measures.

All this need not imply a bureaucratic approach, although a drift towards officialdom is a serious risk that must be guarded against. The intent, rather, is to co-ordinate, to promote concrete action and to stimulate consideration of strategy, with as much delegation of authority as possible. The organisations (trade associations and others) that are now playing a role in the configuration and certification of training must continue to play that role. The fact that the system focuses on the results of training, and especially on ways of achieving those results (training models and types of experience that can be certified), together with an emphasis on requirements and due allowance for future change, will make it an agent of rationalisation by co-ordinating widely dispersed means rather than by concentrating resources in its own hands.

It is of course possible that this result may yet be achieved by the system now being developed. Two factors may help. The legislation already being promulgated views adjustment over time as desirable. Solutions will also have to be rethought in view of the intended link between the on-the-job and academic subsystems. In any event, the former will raise questions needing a broadly consensual response, case by case.

6.   ASSESSMENT, RECOGNITION AND CERTIFICATION

Some relevant problems of evaluation and recognition of skills and qualifications may be mentioned here. The two main considerations in evaluating training are how far actual practice corresponds to the definitions adopted and how relevant the profiles actually produced are to the requirements of an occupation. Separate studies on vocational schools and the apprenticeship system are being carried out by entities independent of the training bodies, involving all participants in the training process. Other researchers are looking at labour force entry and vocational pathways. These studies are expected to produce important information and should help confirm or modify training profiles, assess their quality and legitimise their certification. They will, it is hoped, provide a better understanding of learning processes, and methods and resources may require adjustment.

With respect to learner evaluation, the apprenticeship and vocational education projects have two innovative features. Continuous evaluation will be carried out using a modular approach in which trainees participate and are jointly responsible. In both systems, final exams involve the social partners, either in setting papers or as examiners, in an attempt to link training and work more closely, with co-ordination being required at all stages. The hoped-for result is that training will be better, more useful and more readily certifiable.

In the labour market and the training system alike, the problem of recognition is linked to certification. As already stated, any certified qualification is in our view sufficient to allow the holder to continue his training and go on to higher qualification levels, both at home and in other EU countries. However, access to the higher level may bring with it additional requirements. In Portugal, under the recently instituted system of access to higher education, the secondary diploma is a prerequisite but actual access remains subject to specific tests imposed by the particular institution. Actual recognition varies according to training levels and subsystems, and the whole system is still far from flexible; recognition is particularly problematic where students have not completed a training cycle. This presents difficulties with equivalence that are unlikely to be resolved by certification.

Recognition by the labour market raises different issues, because of the low average level of schooling and the prevalence of skills acquisition through experience. It is now commonplace to say that schooling and occupational training have become devalued, so that less weight is given to the possession of certified qualifications. Even today, many technologically unsophisticated small- and medium-sized businesses do not generally ask for such qualifications, even when the occupation involved requires them and job applicants to possess them. It is essential, therefore, for the social partners to become involved in certification and the configuration of training in order to adapt it to occupational requirements and the needs of the economy. That would give the "products" of the training system a higher profile, and make them sought after, provided that certification is recognised as reflecting quality.

In conclusion, of the three subjects of this paper – evaluation, certification and recognition of vocational skills and qualifications – certification has proved most controversial in Portugal, because of its entry into the European Union, the free movement of workers, and the diversification of training. At the same time, the incipient trend toward regulation of training supply and demand has, at EU level, turned into regulation of occupations; this illustrates the fundamental ambiguity surrounding the purpose and objectives of certification, and not only in Portugal, where a certification system being implemented in 1993 has raised a number of questions and doubts. The looming problem of evaluation, in its various aspects, will soon, no doubt, be an essential concern. Evaluation is a prerequisite if the recognition of skills and qualifications, in particular by the labour market, is to become a universal requirement.

B. REPORTS FROM
THE WORKING GROUP

WORKING GROUP I

THE CURRICULAR AND PEDAGOGIC IMPLICATIONS OF NEW APPROACHES TO ASSESSMENT AND CERTIFICATION

Rapporteur: Michael Young
Institute of Education, University of London

1. THE ISSUES

The priority of purposes over methods

The group first discussed the issue of appropriate methods of assessment. For example, is it desirable that written tests, common in academic (or general) education, be used in vocational programmes? It is important that the choice of method correspond with the objectives of assessment in each case. Such objectives include encouraging progression to higher levels, accrediting prior experience as the basis for adults returning to study or assessing a candidate's suitability for a particular job. Thus, each case requires a different method of assessment.

Likewise, competence in different occupational areas and at different levels will need to be assessed by different methods. Two examples illustrate this point: first, some occupations require a much greater emphasis on oral skills than others, and second, whereas evidence for a low-level practical skill might be obtained from an employee's performance in the work place, a much more elaborate assessment is necessary to identify whether the same employee has the potential to take on greater responsibilities or is capable of higher levels of study.

The importance of taking account of national traditions and experience

Assessment methods and issues hold a different significance in the context of each country. Some nations have long traditions of assessment by the teachers themselves, while others have depended on external examining bodies. Likewise, some countries have highly developed systems of collaboration between employers, employee organisations and teachers, through which considerable mutual trust is established between the partners. In others, this trust barely exists. It is not surprising in the latter case that there is a greater emphasis on external modes of assessment.

New combinations of skills and knowledge

Regardless of their history and present circumstances, all OECD countries are faced with similar pressures from the increasingly competitive global economy. New forms of production are demanding new levels of skill and new combinations of skills and knowledge. It was therefore natural to ask what these new competences were and how and by whom they might be assessed. There was general agreement on the following points:

- While individual firms inevitably give priority to their short-term needs and therefore to specific skills, their competitiveness in the longer term will depend on the broader and more generic capacities of their employees. Governments must be aware that these conflicts of interest are inevitable and they should not assume that because employers are only interested in their immediate skill needs, longer-term and more general skills are unimportant (for national economies as well as for the survival of individual firms).

- Nobody can be certain what new skills will be needed. However, it is clear that skills will change more quickly than in the past, workers at all levels will need to be adaptable and open to change and, in the future, there will increasingly be emphasis on new *processes* (learning to learn and take risks, and developing problem-solving skills) rather than new *contents*.

- It is important that those involved in education and training be specific when defining "generic" skills. A number of countries attempted unsuccessfully to introduce (and assess) forms of general education as a component of vocational education programmes.

2. RECOMMENDATIONS AND PROPOSALS

Recommendations relate specifically to the impact of current changes in work organisation, and the need to create new incentives for young people to take vocational courses. Training programmes are increasingly required to encourage the flexibility and responsibility of employees, rather than just their capacity to demonstrate specific skills. Furthermore, they are encouraged to take on young people who previously would have left school or college for unskilled work. These demands create new problems for teachers and for those designing assessment methods.

The impact of changes in work organisation

- Assessment of the new kinds of "process" skills have to relate to specific work contexts as well as demonstrating the capacity of students/trainees to be analytical. Such assessment cannot be carried out by teachers or employers alone but through partnerships between them. It is important therefore that both OECD and national governments disseminate examples of successful co-operation in this field.

- Employers, individually, in local groups and in their associations, must be encouraged to participate in assessment at both the design and the implementation stages. The credibility of assessment methods depends on the support of employers. This is particularly true of approaches based on portfolios and records of achievement. Such methods, often widely accepted by teachers, make far greater demands on employers' time than conventional methods; employers need to be actively involved from the beginning if they are to be convinced of their value.

- VOTEC programmes need to develop in the future not only skills and knowledge but *attitudes to work* (for example, the ability to take responsibility and to work without supervision). These are important even if they are not as amenable to assessment.

- As VOTEC programmes become more flexible and students/trainees are given greater responsibility to create their own programmes from a large range of modules, the role of career guidance specialists becomes crucial. Career guidance officers should play an integral role in course design and the implementation of programmes.

- Support must be given to teachers to develop new learning approaches and assessment methods that draw on as wide a variety of contexts as possible. In particular, they need to find ways of enabling students/trainees to evaluate their own learning strategies.

- In light of the new demands being made on teachers and the difficulty of combining rather than opposing didactic and learner-centred pedagogies, consideration should be given to new approaches to the preparation of teachers, that involve both the institutions providing training, and the colleges in which vocational courses are offered.

- As a way of defining broader generic skills, OECD countries are encouraged to regroup occupations into larger categories as a basis for foundation vocational programmes.

- Parallel to this clustering of occupational areas, employers should be encouraged to identify sector training needs as opposed to the specific needs of individual firms or specific, specialised processes.

Creating new incentives for young people (and adults seeking further training) to join vocational programmes
further training) to join vocational programmes

It is important to design motivating vocational programmes for young people (such as the American Tech Prep programme of applied academic studies), by making learning and assessment activities more like "real work" and less like school. This means making them more collective and negotiable and offering greater opportunities for students to improve their level, unlike the typical academic programmes that culminate in a final examination. Opportunities for vertical mobility need to be created, regardless of the level, focus or type of programme (full- or part-time). This can be done by ensuring that all vocational qualifications provide access to higher education. Vocational qualifications need to be built into ladders of *occupational* as well as *educational* progression. This would mean, for example, that dental mechanics could become dentists, and legal and accounting clerks become lawyers and accountants.

Higher education staff need to be informed of the new routes from vocational programmes into higher education, and shown that, with the development of "franchising", the traditional divide between vocational and higher education is giving way to a real continuum.

Proposals for research and development

The working group proposed a comparative research study into the new forms of *general* vocational education that are being developed in a number of OECD countries to replace the traditional alternative between occupationally specific training and academic programmes. Such a study needs to explore the relationship between these new programmes and other routes, their opportunities for progression, and the different approaches they propose to the relationship between general knowledge and vocational specialisation.

The insufficiency of foreign languages in VOTEC programmes constitutes a major barrier to horizontal mobility. The OECD and its Member governments are advised to undertake a study, drawing on the experiences of smaller countries and the immigrant communities of larger countries for whom learning at least one second language is a necessity.

3. CONCLUSION

Some working group participants expressed concern about the consequences of developing distinctive vocational and academic tracks for 16 to 19-year-olds, rather than an integrated system in which students could follow a range of pathways through different combinations of theoretical and applied modules. As general vocational programmes are developed and as students are encouraged to make choices in terms of their long-term vocational aims rather than competing for places in traditional high-status (academic) programmes, there is less and less reason for separate tracks with distinct assessment systems. Such a conclusion holds different implications for those countries with tried and tested VOTEC systems and those currently developing them.

WORKING GROUP II

THE ROLE OF ASSESSMENT AND CERTIFICATION IN THE FUNCTIONING OF TRAINING AND LABOUR MARKETS

Rapporteur: Myriam Campinos-Dubernet
GIP - Mutations industrielles, Paris
(CEREQ, Paris, at the time of the Porto seminar)

INTRODUCTION

Most countries recognise a need for certification, including countries whose predominant form of training is apprenticeship. Certification is a way of assessing the training outcome against a standard equivalent, to which any qualifications awarded can be referred. This means, of course, that both training and assessment conditions must be reasonably homogeneous.

However, the standard equivalent principle can only work on the labour market if both sides of industry effectively recognise the certification system that has been established. On the employers' side, certification involves a presumption that the individual holding an award will in fact be competent. Hiring practices confirm employers' confidence in the certification system, as does the recognition that is implied when certification is used as a basis for wage bargaining. What employees and trade unions both want is clear recognition for the certification system, as a guarantee that the emphasis on training at the recruitment stage will definitely pay off.

Thus, certification and its recognition in any one society help define a "validity area" for a given qualification. However, no labour market is ever set for good. It is constantly changing, both over time and over space.

Firstly, the labour market is shaped by institutional mechanisms reflecting mobility patterns and the certification systems used. The latter are broader in a country whose internal labour market predominates (Japan and to a lesser degree France). They are vocational in countries like Germany and the United Kingdom in which external markets are influential.

Secondly, the labour market is subject to processes of change, which are associated with economic developments (e.g. in the technological or organisational fields) influencing the supply of employment opportunities. It is also affected by any changes in the demand for employment that may be associated with demography or with training availability.

Apart from these trends, which are mainly caused by changing labour-use patterns and changing factors of mobility within a given geographical area, the way in which certification relates to the labour market is also influenced by changes in the area. The building of a European labour market is an unprecedented event in this connection.

Changing labour-use patterns are of great concern to all parties involved in training, to the extent that significant changes in how labour markets operate, and the public debate about the role and functioning of vocational training, focus attention on these patterns and identify any problems arising from them.

Mobility is an aspect which people regard, rightly or wrongly, as being less urgent although relevant for the future.

I. HOW CAN CERTIFICATION ADAPT TO LABOUR MARKET TRENDS?

It is widely recognised that certification must keep up with developments in the lives of individuals and firms.

The concept of vocational training

Such adaptability to change depends very largely on how people perceive vocational training. This is why it must be based on general as well as vocational knowledge.

However, while the working group generally agrees on that principle, the significance attached to it varies widely from one country to another. This appears to be wholly bound up with whatever institutional background one sets the principle against, and is not a matter of the status of employers, employees or instructors. Socio-economic background, combined with awareness of the difficulties and options facing every system, in fact accounted for the various concepts of what we call general knowledge, *i.e.* the concepts that can help to make a certification system adaptable. For example:

- A country such as the United Kingdom, whose overall vocational education system has a schooling component that is comparatively less well developed and was only recently made compulsory, defines general competences very broadly as "core skills" – being able to communicate, solve problems, etc.
- For a country like France, where school-based training predominates and perhaps actually sets the tone in vocational training – schools largely define

the system's diplomas and assessment procedures and themselves carry out assessment (even for apprenticeship, considered as a minor form of vocational training) – general knowledge is a matter of scientific and technological skills.

– Countries with a genuine dual system, *i.e.* German-speaking countries and some in Northern Europe (including the Netherlands and Denmark – though not Finland, whose system resembles the French one) define general knowledge as the product of fully successful vocational training. The success of such training determines individuals' capacity to adapt to changes encountered over a working lifetime, and industry's ability to adapt to the necessary changes in the use of labour.

It follows that the apparent consensus that general training can respond to changing labour markets masks ideas of how to make it responsive that are utterly different, if not indeed divergent.

In a rather similar way, countries agreed on the need for a certification system to favour adaptability by offering the individual a career development opportunity throughout his or her working lifetime. Here again, though, it was those countries in which the linkage between initial and continuous training is either the most problematical (United Kingdom, Australia) or where the two compete (France), that attached most importance to this aspect. On the other hand, a country like Germany, where the two are currently better meshed and thereby actually help to structure the way in which the labour market functions, tends to regard the need for certification to favour adaptability as self-evident.

How can vocational training be made adaptable and responsive to change?

The key to making vocational training adaptable seems to be to define profiles that are not unduly narrow, nor too specific. Most countries hoped to move their systems towards broader categories of occupational profiles for certification. Hungary, for example, has cut the number of its trade groups from 40 to 15 families. Denmark has reduced its occupational profiles six-fold, cutting down the number from 300 to 50. Germany implemented substantial reform during the 1970s, and France moved along the same lines during the 1980s.

Ways of adapting certification to changing labour markets vary widely from one country to another, with patterns directly reflecting each country's institutional structures. For dual-system countries, ongoing communication between all sides in any one occupational branch (representatives of employers, trade unions, education authorities) seems the obvious course and is standard practice.

In a country like France, where the schooling component predominates, education authorities play a special role in that they implement a comprehensive vocational training policy. Although a variety of bodies have responsibility for organising relations with the parties concerned, their role is only advisory. What is difficult is how to give a fresh spur to whatever policy has been decided upon, which implies some measure of standardisation while still respecting the problems encountered in the various industries, whose traditions and expectations are never identical.

Conversely, in countries such as the United Kingdom and Australia, where the conventional apprenticeship has long been the predominant form of vocational training, and interest in certification has only developed recently, relations between the parties concerned are far more adversarial. The challenge here is to transform all this into a dual kind of system, involving not only certification but also some compulsory school-based training on top of whatever firms may be providing. Introducing certification where there has been none before may have the effect of making workers potentially more mobile. This presupposes that companies training and using manpower are abiding by the same rules: instead of some having the fruits of their investment poached away by others, each one should make its contribution to the training effort.

In whatever way countries may be approaching vocational training – except in an internal market country like Japan – where it is the user firm which has sole responsibility for vocational training there seems to be general agreement that the majority of firms cannot predict what their longer-term needs will be. Employers' representatives are perhaps in a better position to do so. However, in many countries the question does arise of reconciling the differing interests expressed by larger and smaller firms *vis-à-vis* the same trades and occupations. For example, larger companies can more readily accommodate an "adaptable profile" and go on to tailor that profile to their own specific requirements. Smaller firms need profiles that they can make use of more quickly.

Thus, the varied and indeed diverging interests of industry, employees and education authorities suggest that whatever approach may be taken to vocational training, it is unrealistic to expect a consensus. Conversely, achieving some genuine compromise among all these interests is clearly essential, since it is likely to lead to constructive solutions that are future-oriented. Sudden, "revolutionary" shifts in certification systems are liable to prove short-lived.

Looking beyond more immediate aims and the rather varied approaches to attaining those goals, what has so far been achieved in response to changing labour markets?

Certain countries, like Germany and others with fairly similar systems, are tending to adapt the content of existing diplomas, sometimes after exhaustive negotiation over as long as several years to achieve an acceptable compromise.

France, conversely, has made very sweeping changes to its vocational training system over five years (1985-1990). It was not just a matter of combining a certain number of training pathways and updating the content of existing diplomas to meet changing technology. A new diploma, the vocational baccalaureate, introduced at the request of one industry, metal-working, has been extended throughout industry. The role of the existing vocational diploma, the CAP (*Certificat d'aptitude profes-sionnel*), previously the benchmark for entry to skilled blue- and white-collar jobs, and for collective bargaining between the two sides of industry, has been called into question. France implemented this policy by altering the guidance system in general education, as part of a decision to bring 80 per cent of every age group to baccalaureate level.

Canada, in contrast with other countries, seems to be adopting a continuous process of certification designed to assess any individual so requesting. A special feature of the process is that it not only allows for vocational experience from initial and continuing training but also for work experience. This approach is intended to encourage labour market mobility for individuals with several different backgrounds and mixed profiles via a clear identification system enabling the employer to recognise what the individuals concerned can do. The system was thought by some members of the working group to be cumbersome, costly and perhaps bureaucratic.

Looking beyond the variety of ways in which certification has been tailored to potential change, two points emerge:

- The first relates to work experience. There is genuine consensus that the work situation, and experience in industry, play a central role in training. In countries where industries play a major role in training, that much is self-evident. It is less so in those countries in which school-based training has traditionally predominated. The cost of new technologies, and the conditions for using them efficiently, have both considerably altered the standpoints of those who have favoured relying exclusively on the schools.

- The second, broader point is that there can be no cure-all. Trends in certification involve some complex social processes. They are therefore bound to clash. The only general principle in this area, on which there is a wide consensus, is that the institution designing certification should not be the same as the one assessing it.

2. CERTIFICATION AND MOBILITY

The value of certification is in providing a credible, trustworthy benchmark for all concerned within any given area for mobility. There is admittedly some danger when that benchmark becomes untrustworthy as a result of change, so that it comes to seem insufficiently authoritative. But however countries are approaching their certification process, the most important point is that if changes in it do prove to be necessary, they must be the outcome of compromise.

The reason for this is that certification is like money, and what matters is that all concerned believe in it. It is trust, being confident that some qualification really is worth having, which is what ultimately validates the certification process. That trust on the part of all concerned is what makes certification a genuine benchmark for mobility. If individuals themselves have helped build up the system, so that it is not just one that someone else has offered them, their trust will be even greater. But that is where the analogy with money no longer applies.

We can summarise the problem partly by looking into how the links between "certification" and "qualification" come to be forged, and then at how the links between "certification", "qualification" and "remuneration" are forged. This progressive approach makes sense because things become very different depending on whether we look at all three terms in the relationship, or whether we look only at the first two.

How certification relates to qualification

Not everyone agrees on how certification relates to qualification. Two difficulties can crop up. The first is a need to establish just *what it is we are trying to qualify* – the job or the individual. If certification is attached to the individual, it clearly makes sense to attach the qualification to the individual as well. This is generally how the employees' representatives see it.

However, if the qualification certified does not match the profile of the job on offer or of the work position, there will be a problem. It is only fair to take features of the work position into account too. That is the employers' standpoint.

It is nevertheless possible to identify a common ground. It would clearly be unreasonable to dismiss out of hand any need for "certification/qualification" to match the work position. All concerned, including employees' representatives, are nowadays coming to understand this.

The second difficulty is in *defining the qualification itself.* Ought it to be defined in close detail, or might something broader be more useful?

A precise qualification has the advantage that it allows for a definition which identifies all the training received (initial plus further training) as well as work experience. Even so, it has the disadvantage of being cumbersome and costly to maintain, some people seeing it as involving too much red tape. Canada's experience mentioned above is a typical example.

Conversely, most countries felt that these relations should preferably be broad. That was partly because broader relations would keep pace with the present trend for training to widen its own profiles, in the interests of facilitating mobility both in movement and over time (reflecting the difficulty of anticipating all future change). But broader relations would also match a trend towards organising work more flexibly, in response alike to gradual change on the demand side (shorter product life-cycles) and to make optimum use of new kinds of equipment, which can often be used most efficiently for as long as possible if the user has a fairly all-round profile.

How do certification, qualification and remuneration relate to one another?

Just as some compromise clearly emerged on the previous issue, standpoints diverged strongly on the question of how certification, qualification and remuneration should relate to one another. These differing views mainly reflected where the parties concerned happened to stand in the system, rather than the situation in their country.

Employers' representatives, for instance, expressed anxiety that too close a link between all three might have the effect of unduly rigidifying their scope for managing their work forces. While conceding that there might be benefits in facilitating expectations and levelling the rules for competition among employers, too close a link might deprive employers of their discretion to assess the individual's actual abilities, insofar as the standard certification did not fully express those abilities.

On the other side, employees and their representatives made the point that close links were what made it possible to ascertain in advance how much they could anticipate from possessing a recognised qualification. The employee's interest was to protect his earnings, just as it was to the employee's advantage, and not to the employer's, for his qualification to be scarce.

Interestingly, this latter point applies more to countries in which the supply of training is closely determined by the labour market situation. In fact, several countries nowadays have introduced ways of ensuring a degree of continuity in the supply of training by stepping in to adapt the availability of training places.

This depends more especially on what the institutional rules happen to be in any one country. Apart from that, such diverging views as were expressed transcended situations in individual countries to depend entirely on where the speaker happened to stand in the system: employers and employees see the certification/remuneration relationship in a fundamentally different way.

Certification and the area in which it applies

Very wide consensus emerged on the area in which any given certification should apply. In awareness of existing institution differences between one country and another, it was agreed that for the time being, the areas in which certification should apply ought still to be individual countries.

Two points were made to support this:

- First, confining the area in that way is not nowadays much of a brake on workers' mobility from country to country, as witness movements of frontier workers, which take place easily enough already.

– Second, the issue is sensitive, and therefore no rapid change can be expected.

Although the Brussels authorities have been concerned with this question for many years now, both employers and employees feel that there is no need to make haste. This consensus shows what a complex issue this is, since shifting the focus from certification to job profiles would clearly do nothing to simplify the intricate problem. It is difficult to see how this might result in any kind of workable document that the general public could readily consult.

WORKING GROUP III

PORTABILITY AND TRANSFERABILITY OF QUALIFICATIONS

Rapporteur: Mr. Prostes Da Fonseca
Ministry of Education, Lisbon, Portugal

INTRODUCTION

A distinction needs to be made between several kinds of transferability, for qualifications and for the certificates attesting them. To begin with, transferability may refer to *functions* or *work positions* (which may imply a change of occupation between areas whose definitions are distinct though the skills involved are similar – as in typing and word processing by a secretary, and typesetting by a printer. Transferability may also refer to *areas* of activity (perhaps also involving some change of occupational status or remuneration because of collective bargaining). It may refer to *regions* (leading to new working practices, as in the construction industry), and even to different *countries*, then involving formal or legal recognition of certificates.

The "portability" concept perhaps applies more readily to the geographical or area dimension, while transferability refers to different kinds of work. At this point we may disregard the problem of transferability for qualifications within different training and educational streams and, in particular, the problem of the transition from academic to vocational streams and *vice versa*.

All agree that transferability is an issue that must be seen against the background of socio-economic development policies, and that it has to be enlightened by principles of sound human resource management. The mobility implying that qualifications be recognised as transferable is not an end in itself. What it represents is the economics of qualifications as one dimension in overall development policy. It helps individuals to find employment elsewhere when jobs are no longer available in their own geographical or sectoral area, or it helps attract to some given place or sector the skilled manpower needed to develop a particular economic project. So transferability is not just of concern to the individual as a worker, or to the employer as responsible for any given undertaking, but also to every local and regional authority which is keen to have every asset to hand that may be needed in developing human resources within the area for which it is responsible.

From that standpoint, transferability policy should be able to consider the full range of skills that people may have acquired, not just the formal aspect of an initial certificate. Transferability concerns personal qualifications, and hence covers all acquired skills including those derived from training and those added later through work experience.

Although straightforward methods, principles and procedures must be used for achieving transferability in order to meet the same requirements described elsewhere concerning the conditions governing the credibility of certification (given that recognition of certificates by employers is the whole purpose of the certification exercise), the attempt to achieve credibility through straightforward means should not be made to the detriment of special cases. In the first place, transferability affects individuals: it must therefore respect each specific case and be open to the diversity of specific situations.

The introduction of measures encouraging transferability should take into account those ultimately concerned, *i.e.* those who are directly affected and involved in the proposed procedures. These are not just the employers alone but all the individuals for whom recognition of their qualifications is but one of the many problems they have to face in a context of mobility.

A transferability policy (because it must embrace all possible dimensions) requires a very close and permanent dialogue between all parties concerned, *i.e.* social partners (employers and trade unions) as well as training institutions.

Where possible, over-regulated approaches should be avoided, since any system involving controls and excessively detailed procedures would have the opposite effect on mobility than that which transferability is supposed to encourage. Procedures must therefore be found that will guarantee full transparency of situations and clearly show the interaction between supply (qualifications and available skills) on the one hand, and the needs of occupational sectors, regions or countries (demand) on the other.

Of course, full transparency must not overlook cultural, social and linguistic differences, which all hinder mobility over and beyond the problem of specific recognition of professional qualifications.

I. THE "INDIVIDUAL PORTFOLIO" OR THE "WORKER'S PASSPORT" AS A TRANSFERABILITY TOOL

The "individual portfolio" can be considered as a useful transferability tool. It is a document bearing all pertinent information on the "qualifying" experience of the person, and the conditions under which he acquired further experience after obtaining the basic diploma, whether or not connected with the obtention of the latter. This information tool not only favours transferability by informing those whom it may concern about the experience acquired but also takes mobility into account as part and parcel of individual expertise. The fact that experience has been accumulated introduces a "dynamic" aspect into the approach of qualifications, which may take on more importance during a period of change, while this is not always possible through formal certification.

The "portfolio" and its progressive expansion can also fulfil a double role, leading to better evaluation of individual skills both by the employer and by the worker himself:

– It is a useful evaluation tool for employers when the person concerned enters the labour market.

– It represents a considerable self-evaluation aid for the worker, who is thus in a better position to understand the pattern of his own qualifications. Self-evaluation is the first step towards sustained self-training, ensuring continuous career advancement.

The use of the "portfolio" should, of course, lead to the dismissal of a number of unresolved problems. The relationship between its contents and the formal references to the education system must be very clearly set out, precisely because of the role that formal certification continues to play. The first consequence can be important, since the fact that the portfolio relates to an individual removes it from the hierarchical and salary categories supported through collective bargaining and therefore might isolate workers not belonging to them. Most of the social legislation on qualifications in Member countries refers to formal qualifications, which may weaken the use of the portfolio. Lastly, public administration traditionally only uses formal diplomas as criteria for endorsing qualifications. In view of the latest developments in the labour market, it is well known that this factor is still decisive in many countries.

2. TRANSNATIONAL TRANSFERABILITY (EUROPEAN AND OTHER)

Here, artificial rules and regulations should above all be avoided, since they would make the "transnational" labour market even more rigid than many national ones. Mobility, whose social, cultural and personal aspects are so important, is not improved by pinpointing ideal conditions for its operation.

Whilst suitable circumstances must be created for full information about supply and demand in this transnational market to be available and comprehensible, transparency is frequently a more urgent issue than the establishment of precise mobility conditions. In fact, this is what is often requested by social partners in this area. The establishment of transparency, however, should not overlook the fact that the individual moving from one country to another is the subject of the move, and cannot always remain bound up by the formal "labels" which traditional labour markets tend to put on qualifications.

A first step towards transparency might consist in attempting to define a common terminology facilitating transferability. In spite of cultural differences, it should be possible to agree on a number of concepts which, by promoting the ruling of certain essential ideas, would help elucidate real cultural differences.

3. CONCLUSION

Transferability of diplomas entails not their harmonisation but an improved understanding of their differences and originality. It is by encouraging mutual understanding through shared terminology that cultural diversities will be best respected. This is a first step towards broader and more useful exploitation of diversities between countries. Specialised international organisations can play a vital role in this field.

The importance of continuing education in any study on qualifications and their progress in individual careers should be emphasized. This concern will lead to a more flexible definition of qualifications in general and certification in particular.

Taking continuous training into account, as well as what has been mentioned above about the important role of the "portfolio" in self-evaluation and the rising trend towards self-training, it is clear that any individual should be directly involved in his own assessment and should even participate actively in the certification process relating to him. The individual as well as the formal structure responsible for his qualifications, a trade union or a trade association, should be partners in the evaluation exercise and the development of transferability policies. In this way, he will become more independent and better capable of advancing on his own initiative. This is undoubtedly the approach which will best integrate vocational training, with all its implications for career planning and management by the individual concerned, into policies relating not only to education in society in general but also to employment.

WORKING GROUP IV

IMPLEMENTING ASSESSMENT, CERTIFICATION AND VALIDATION

Rapporteur: John Rodgers
Trade Union Congress, London

This group focused on three main themes: identification of the policy challenges, the means for implementing assessment, and recommendations on policies to pursue in the future.

1. IDENTIFICATION OF THE POLICY CHALLENGES

From the outset there was agreement that the goals of assessment must be made clear and that these must be defined so that the aims followed correspond with overall vocational training policy and its relationship with the education system.

One of the central challenges facing many OECD countries is to distinguish, on the one hand, the traditional role of selection that assessment plays in the academic school system and, on the other (given the trends of young people to remain in the education system for longer periods and the greater diversity of needs, capabilities and aspirations), to extend the range of vocational training options open to them, which should in turn expand opportunities for employment and career development.

Another challenge can be seen in the measures taken by several OECD countries to develop structures of assessment and qualifications that aim at setting national standards of quality. Efforts should be made to resolve the tensions between creating flexible and responsive structures of certification and qualification that promote greater access for all, and ensuring that they remain coherent and efficient. Keeping in mind the complexity of the issue, efforts for progress in implementing assessment, certification and validation mechanisms should aim to produce a more qualified, highly skilled work force. An additional policy challenge is implementing structures at reas onable cost, with acceptable "trade-offs".

The working group also underlined the importance of creating a structure that allows for the active participation of unions and employers, meets the needs of young people and adults, and addresses the issue of uncertified skills through accreditation of prior learning.

2.   IMPLEMENTATION OF ASSESSMENT

The concept of a continuum between academic and vocational education (such as that proposed by Sheila Clarke and Ron Tuck earlier in this volume) is considered to be a better model than the traditional pattern of complete separation. Flexibility would be greatly increased through a modular approach to education, providing a variety of pathways for people of all ages and ability levels. Access must also be made more flexible, since people also learn outside schools.

In designing programmes for the implementation of assessment, certification and validation, the following objectives need to be considered:

– ensuring that education and learning needs are met;

– meeting labour market and employment requirements.

Can the process of assessment be designed to meet both these goals? And, if so, are two types of certification required? In addition, it is necessary to provide a formative assessment with good feedback to the students. It was also recognised that the concept of assessment should be considered in broader terms to include:

– education/trainer assessment;

– industrial/employer/social partner assessment;

– team assessment;

– self-assessment.

Another key factor in designing an assessment system is to determine whether the ultimate aim is excellence – making good better – or competence. On this point there was some disagreement over the philosophy of approach. The disadvantage of an excellence approach is that the assessment process risks becoming distorted as it moves into the area of values, attitudes, or cultural bias, which could become very complicated and costly. On the other hand, it was argued that if assessors, whoever they were, did not assess beyond competence, others in the labour market would.

There were also misconceptions about the competence-based approach in terms of its broad aims and scope. A competence-based approach is concerned with promoting minimum standards and generally improving those presently existing in many occupations; it encourages individuals to progress beyond minimum standards set at various levels. It is important, however, that an approach emphasizing outcomes should not lose sight of inputs, particularly their quality and ways of assuring and delivering them.

The group also felt that justice could not be done to implementing new assessment systems without a regard for cost. A range of options should therefore be available based on judgements concerning cost-effectiveness, cost-efficiency and access. But it was recognised that there could be tensions between cost-efficiency and access. Furthermore, assessment is complex and often has several meanings. Assessment of student performance, for example, not only reveals student achievement but provides information on the quality of the teachers, trainers or the teaching methods used.

An important issue is the necessity for anonymity to pursue an objective assessment process, and public authorities should ensure such methods are open to public scrutiny.

Assessment systems, industry and employment which involve the social partners (unions and employers) in the design and implementation process, present an advantage insofar as they are directly concerned with the results of the system in terms of employment and the dynamism of changes. Public accreditation of institutions/bodies awarding certification is also an important issue in the assessment process.

Finally, all key players – providers and consumers – must feel comfortable with the assessment system, otherwise any attempts at innovation will prove difficult.

3. POLICY RECOMMENDATIONS

In the debate on the implementation of assessment systems much attention has focused on the concept itself and policy design issues but very little on implementation of strategies. This applies not only to responding to change but encouraging it.

Some OECD countries have recently developed innovations in the field of qualifications and related assessment systems, especially those inspired by competence-based approaches. Other forms of innovation have also received strong political support. Nevertheless, the evidence available suggests that the success of such innovations depends on the understanding and support of the involved agencies for the changes under way.

Well-meaning policies often have unintended consequences or reveal weaknesses when implemented. Thus, implementation strategies must also focus on successful and effective delivery at all levels. Policy design alone is not sufficient: without strategies that engage, convince and secure the support of the key players (teachers, trainers, assessors, the social partners, consumers) for the innovations that are to take place, there is considerable risk that desirable policy objectives will not be realised. In conclusion, the working group recommended special policy studies to draw lessons for effective strategies of implementing reforms.

Part II

COUNTRY CASE STUDIES

AUSTRIA

ISSUES OF CERTIFICATION IN THE DUAL SYSTEM

by

Helmut Aigner †
Federal Ministry of Education, Vienna

1. PRELIMINARY REMARKS

Vocational assessment shares many of the parameters and problems that characterise other forms of assessment. These fall into the broad areas of:

– standards to be applied;

– examination methods;

– evaluation scales.

There are basically three types of standards against which a person's achievement can be measured:

– externally defined *objectives* (e.g. a given speed and a predefined error rate in making routine bookkeeping entries);

– the *mean achievement* of some representative group (anything between a class of students and the entire population of a nation);

– the *margin of achievement* gained by a student between the start and the termination of a course.

At first glance, assessment by objectives appears to be the most useful method for practical purposes: an employer or the director of an advanced programme would want to know whether (or how well) a candidate has mastered certain specific knowledge and skills. However, what is he or she to do if all or none of the candidates satisfy the requirements? A programme which regularly leads to such extreme results is indeed likely to have its formal objectives changed so that they become achievable by the majority of students. A further problem of assessment by achievement is the sheer mass of individual objectives for which, ideally, achievement would have to be evaluated.

Assessment by mean achievement has the opposite drawbacks. What help is it to know whether a candidate's achievement is in the second or third quartile of his or her class, if the level of the class mean with respect to required knowledge and skills is undefined and may indeed vary widely from one class to another? Basing assessment on a national mean would be very costly and still solve only part of the problem unless reference to specific objectives was made.

Assessment by margin of achievement may be the best way to measure the effectiveness of a programme and thus contribute to improvements in programme design and teaching methods. But for external purposes this principle has several drawbacks: it necessitates examinations both at the start and at the end of a programme; it fails in the case of students who start the programme with nearly all the knowledge and skills it is designed to impart; it is misleading in the case of students whose achievement has been enhanced from very poor to merely unsatisfactory; and it is not applicable at all to candidates who wish to have their previous self-learned knowledge assessed.

It will thus be seen that none of the three principles, carried to its logical extreme, is ultimately useful or socially acceptable; in practice, therefore, some mixture of the principles must be applied. This seems all the more justified as a) most examiners are not aware of the principles and b) the attainable precision of measurement that would be required for obtaining reliable predictors is sadly limited in most cases. It is not unusual for employers to overtly or subconsciously look at diplomas not so much for the achievements they profess to document but as evidence that a candidate has demonstrated the stamina and frustration tolerance which are required to "stick out a tough programme" and will also stand him in good stead in the job at hand. Be that as it may, the officially proclaimed principle of assessment in Austria is by objectives, tempered in practice by the above considerations.

Examination methods may be categorised as follows:

– written, oral or practical;

– essay-type *vs.* objective.

If assessment is based on coursework, the following further classification is desirable:

– examination by programme teachers *vs.* outside examiners;

– continuous assessment *vs.* end-of-programme examination.

The assessment of *skills* must obviously be based on a demonstration of the skills concerned, thus requiring practical examinations. Where it is a question of communicative skills, the choice of written and/or oral examinations is also obvious. It is the domain of *knowledge* where the question of written *vs.* oral examinations is controversial. Written examinations have been proved, *ceteris paribus*, to be more economical and to yield more reliable results than the oral type. The latter, on the other hand, are better in avoiding misunderstandings between examiner and examinee; if performed as part of coursework, it makes for a better class atmosphere, does somewhat better in discouraging sole reliance on the lecture method and can in itself, through the examination dialogue, provide a learning experience. Any combination of the two types is possible, and the balance will depend on the relative importance that programme designers assign to the various advantages cited above.

The essay-type question and its oral equivalent seem particularly suitable for situations where a combination of factual knowledge and logical and communicative skills is to be demonstrated. They are comparatively easy to prepare but take all the longer to evaluate, particularly where the merits of different papers are to be compared. The "objective" test with "bound" or short-answer questions is better suited to pinpoint specific knowledge and skills. To be effective, it needs careful preparation based on practice acquired in teacher training. It is quickly evaluated and seldom taxes the conscience of the examiner.

Examination by outsiders goes a long way toward ensuring objective results, since programme teachers who know their students may be swayed by overt or subconscious likes and dislikes, as well as by the desire to show satisfactory success rates. However, such a system is more expensive, it places examinees under greater psychological pressure, it precludes continuous assessment, and the body of previous years' examination questions may tend to acquire greater weight than the formally published syllabus. It seems that in discussing the reform of examinations in a given country, critics frequently aver that switching from whatever is the current system to the other would solve most problems.

There is a whole spectrum of possibilities between evaluating a student's every act during, say, a five-year programme, doing completely without formal examinations, and a system whereby success or failure wholly depends on the student's performance during a few hours or even minutes at the end of a programme.[1] Continuous assessment can, through the sheer number of assessment events, avoid most of the errors of random sampling, and it makes for a more relaxed classroom atmosphere, ideally removing all examination pressure. The teacher, however, is in a dilemma. Unless he keeps a running record, his memory is likely to play tricks on him; but if he does, classroom atmosphere will be poisoned, assessment will take pride of place over instruction, and pressure will be exacerbated rather than relieved. A combined system may feature semi-formal oral tests, short written quizzes and/or hour examinations.

The situation in Austria with respect to the above assessment methods is as follows: the oral examination is, though half-heartedly, decreed to be more valuable than the written type but, in cases of appeal from an assessment, authorities consider examination papers more reliable evidence than whatever witnesses may remember of an oral examination. Hour examinations are only permitted in a handful of subjects, subject to severe limitations of number and duration. The essay-type question is far more prevalent than the objective question, due both to deficiencies in teacher training and perhaps a vague feeling that it may be easier to obtain an acceptable distribution of grades with the help of the subjective components in essay questions. Examination by programme teachers is generally favoured over outside examiners, unless there has not been a previous programme. Continuous assessment has the official favour (again provided there is a programme). Exceptions to the above generalisations will be noted where they are pertinent.

The gap between expectations and what an assessment system can actually deliver is largest in the domain of grading. The trouble is that grades are expected at the same time to give detailed information about a person's achievement in meeting dozens of objectives that may be of relevance for further study and/or productive work and to wrap them all up neatly in a single letter or number which will magically convey all that is needed for a hiring or admissions decision. Thus, grading systems have been developed between the poles of *comprehensiveness* and *itemisation*, as well as between *formal scales* and *verbal assessment*.

Imagine a brave new world where a student's diploma consists of a plastic card on which everything he has shown himself capable of doing is encoded. The profile of requirements for a job or for a subsequent programme is similarly coded, and the recruitment officer's job is taken over by a computer and an input slot for the "vocational credit card". Aside from the philosophical objections to such a horror scenario, it could only be reliable if the database were of enormous size, which in turn would require assessment procedures both comprehensive and perfect in validity and reliability. Somehow an algorithm taking into account deterioration of knowledge and skills with time (unless kept up by practice) would also have to be worked in.

The state of the art of pedagogical psychology is such that the desired degree of precision in assessment cannot be obtained; even if it could, the time for preparation and administration of the required tests, as well as the cost of implementing such a system, would be prohibitive. It is therefore not surprising that the grading system practised in a given country's school system should come under frequent public attack. (There is less public interest in assessment outside schools.) In Austria, where, by and large, diplomas show a global grade, suggestions frequently voiced include:

– doing without grades altogether;

– substituting verbal assessment for the grade scale;

– making grades somehow more valid and more reliable.[2]

Aside from the practical difficulties they present, all these proposals have a "progressive" flavour, thus causing conservative opinion to oppose them; in a country where a modification of the grading system would require a two-thirds majority in parliament, this fact alone precludes any radical change.

Abolition of grades would, at least for vocational purposes, create the necessity of post-school assessment, which would run up against the same difficulties as the system it would supplant. It is therefore not surprising that "alternative" schools that do without grades do not exist in the vocational domain.

The problems with verbal assessment are:

- It is more difficult to evaluate as a basis for yes/no decisions on hiring or admission.
- Cliché phrases which are hardly more informative than a grade (*e.g.* "must work harder") tend to be developed.
- Social pressure may work toward suppression of wordings considered detrimental to a person's further chances, so that a system of coded euphemisms may develop.

The question of improved validity and reliability of assessment will be dealt with below within the national context.

2. SYSTEMS OF VOCATIONAL ASSESSMENT IN AUSTRIA

For purposes of classification of assessment systems, the following types of programmes below tertiary level can be distinguished in Austria:

a) full-time programmes in public and private technical and vocational schools (grades 9 through 13), also equivalent extension programmes and extramural examinations;[3]

b) training under the "dual system" of apprenticeship (grades 10 through 13), consisting of:

- *(b1)* on-the-job training in an enterprise (70 to 80 per cent of the apprentice's time) and
- *(b2)* supplementary instruction in a part-time vocational school (20 to 30 per cent);

c) master craftsman's diplomas;

d) civil service diplomas;

e) *ad hoc* programmes offered by non-recognised private schools, employers and employees' organisations, individual employers, etc.

Programmes and diplomas of types *a)* through *d)* are regulated by public law, whereas only certain general provisions of civil law are applicable to type *e)*.

About one-third of the Austrian population acquires certificates and diplomas of type *a)*, which award privileges at levels ranging from skilled workers to engineering technicians. Fairly detailed regulations about assessment in these programmes are laid down in federal acts and ordinances; they are essentially the same as for general-education programmes. Annual reports are issued on the basis of continuous assessment, punctuated by oral quizzes, brief informal tests and hour exams, all of which must be pre-announced and are subject to various restrictions. No end-of-term examinations are provided. There are five grades, "1" being excellent, "4" passing and "5" failing. Promotion to the next grade is conditional upon passing grades in all compulsory subjects, but failure in up to two subjects may be made up at the beginning of the next school year, and in exceptional cases the period of grade for a single subject may be extended to a year. Reports also show promotion with distinction (essentially on an average of 1.5 or better, all subjects being counted equally, regardless of the number of class hours involved). A lesser degree of distinction in coursework (average between 1.5 and 2) has been defined quite recently after having been in use in final examinations for almost 20 years.

Formal final examinations are provided at the end of most programmes of type *a)*, over and above the report for the final year. They consist of written and oral examinations in seven to eight subjects, some of which are compulsory, while others are elected by the candidate. If both written and oral examinations are taken in the same subject, they count as two examinations. Written examinations are of four to five hours' duration in languages and mathematics, while for technical projects, up to five eight-hour working days are set aside, with considerable time devoted to drafting and/or laboratory work. An oral examination may not take more than 15 minutes.

Examiners in final examinations are the teachers of the last grade. They submit two sets of questions for the written part to the provincial school authority, one of which is returned under seal. At the start of the examination the seal is broken. Oral examinations are chaired by a government inspector, and the public is admitted, though in practice only students of lower grades attend. Oral questions are proposed by the teacher concerned and authorised by the chairperson, who may also ask related questions. Grades are awarded by majority vote of the board on a motion by the examiner, the chairman having only a casting vote.

The diploma shows grades (1 through 5) for each written and oral examination and an overall assessment derived therefrom (passed with major or minor distinction; passed; failed). In case of failure, the examination may be re-taken two or three times, the number of subject failures determining the minimum waiting period between attempts.

Among those vocational schools which do not entitle leavers to university access, some do not provide final examinations, limiting themselves to a final-year report. As the leavers of these schools have of late had reduced chances on the labour market, a bill is currently before parliament that would extend final examinations to such programmes as well.

In an assessment system based on the achievement of objectives rather than an empirical mean, only two grades, pass and fail, should theoretically exist. However, if a single grade is to cover a large range of objectives, finer stepping may be desirable. Several distinct grades are also useful in the preparation of short-lists. This is why – with comparatively brief interludes featuring four and six grades respectively – Austria has always had a five-grade system.

But having five grades based on the meeting of objectives presents far greater problems in the definition of each grade than reference to means and standard deviations in the rival system. (There, however, it is difficult to justify why the cut-off point between passing and failing should come at x rather than y standard deviations.) The dilemma is illustrated by the definitions of grades 2 and 3 in force until 1975:

- *Grade 2*: The student has acquired all the specified knowledge and skill, barring non-essentials.
- *Grade 3*: The student has acquired all essential knowledge and skills (average grade).

Not only are the two definitions virtually identical, but the bracketed rider in the definition of grade 3 contains a reference to population means which in specific instances may well conflict with the body of the definition.

Well aware of these deficiencies, the authorities changed the definitions in 1975. It was found that no meaningful and justifiable boundary lines could be drawn if the grades were seen as a sort of linear measure; therefore, the new definitions are based on two parameters, *viz.* achievement in essentials and in non-essentials. For example, "4" now certifies that the student has mastered the majority of the essentials and any amount (or none) of the non-essentials. This, however, still leaves problems in the definition of both *majority* and *essentials*, the latter not being defined in the syllabi, so that in practice the definitions are widely ignored and grades are awarded mainly according to an intuitive mean-based system. Altogether, the grading system is felt to meet requirements rather poorly, but it is maintained because no rival system seems to promise significant improvement.

Approximately half the population of the country go through vocational training of type *b)*, the dual system, completion of which entails skilled-worker or journeyman status. Assessment in the school portion of this system *(b2)* follows the same rules as for type *a)*, except that no final examination is provided. In the on-the-job portion *(b1)*, there is no assessment by the trainer, but an end-of-apprenticeship examination is administered after the legal period of apprenticeship (two to four years). The examination consists of a theoretical and a practical part, the former being waived if the apprentice can present a report on the last grade of the part-time vocational school with passing grades in all subjects. There are three examiners: the chairman and one other examiner are nominated by employers' organisations, while the remaining examiner is nominated by employees' organisations. Examiners must currently exercise the trade in question and be entitled to train apprentices but are barred from examining their own trainees. One teacher from the trainee's part-time vocational school is permitted to be present but not to take part in the examination.

The theoretical part of the end-of-apprenticeship examination typically consists of three written 80-minute examinations, while the practical part consists of the production of a workpiece within eight hours, followed by a 15-minute oral examination. There are the same five grades as in type a), though their definitions are somewhat different, and the overall assessment lacks the "minor distinction" level. After a failure, the examination may be retaken after a waiting period of three to six months.

According to current trade law, self-employment in certain trades requires a licence, for some of which (artisan) passing a master craftsman's examination, type c) above, is a prerequisite. About 3 per cent of the national population are affected. The examination may not be taken until the candidate has been employed in the trade for 30 months after having passed the end-of-apprenticeship test. The examination typically comprises:

- a theoretical technical section, consisting of a five-hour written part and an oral part of 60 to 90 minutes' duration;
- a section on management and law, consisting of a five-hour written part and an oral part of 20 to 40 minutes' duration;
- a practical section of eight hours' duration.

The composition of the master craftsman's examination board is much the same as for the end-of-apprenticeship examination, except that a fourth examiner is added, who must be qualified in management and law.

Preparatory programmes for the master craftsman's examination may or may not be offered; where they are, assessment procedures are essentially the same as for type (b2), and the theoretical technical section and sometimes also the management and law section of the master craftsman's examination, are waived on successful completion of the programme. Perhaps because of the frequent absence of preparatory programmes, the rate of success in master craftsman's examinations is only 60 per cent, in contrast to well over 90 per cent for all other types of examination.

A bill for considerable amendment to the Austrian Trades Act is currently before parliament; no major changes are, however, proposed in the matters described above.

In most branches of the civil service, both basic and further training programmes are provided. A civil service examination, type d) is taken on completion of a basic training programme. These examinations affect, at a very rough estimate, 5 per cent of the national population. Depending on the nature of the civil service post, parts of each examination subject may take the following forms, though at least one written and one oral part are compulsory:

- preparation of a thesis;

- written examination;

- oral examination;

- practical examination.

The examining board consists of a chairperson and at least one further examiner. Active civil servants are allowed to be present. The board either passes or fails the candidate; in the case of a pass, distinction in one, several or all examination subjects may be awarded. The waiting period for re-taking the examination after a failure depends on the frequency of examinations, but cannot be longer than a year.

While the Austrian public places great value on official certificates and diplomas, there are also plenty of *ad hoc* training programmes, type *e)* organised by employers' and employees' associations and by individual employers, without formal regulation by law. On completion of these programmes, in some cases no formal document is issued, while in others only attendance is certified. Where there is a form of assessment, experience with systems *a)* through *e)* usually causes programme organisers to select one of these types or a combination thereof.

3. THE STATUS OF CERTIFICATES AND DIPLOMAS

All certificates and diplomas for programmes *a)* through *d)* carry official status. Private schools wishing to issue such documents need official recognition by the Education Ministry, a procedure dependent on their complying with the same regulations (*e.g.* syllabi, teacher qualification, inspection) as the public schools. Absence of this privilege is probably the main reason why non-recognised private schools play a negligible role in the Austrian education system.

Official status of certificates and diplomas means that:

- Access to the next higher level of education and training (up to university) is granted without further examinations or selection procedures.[4]

- Access to certain occupations (at certain levels) is limited by law to the holders of official documents.

- The grade at which a candidate is admitted into the civil service and – barring further training – the maximum grade he or she can achieve after acquiring appropriate seniority, depends on the certificates or diplomas acquired.

   – No one is allowed to issue documents that could be confused with official certificates or diplomas.

In the private sector of the economy, the formal or informal status and the pay of staff are often dependent on vocational levels ("skilled worker", "foreman", "master craftsman", "engineering technician") as certified by official documents, though an employer is free to hire staff without formal qualification. The vocational levels are also frequently the point of departure in collective bargaining.[5] They can serve as a yardstick for vocational qualification in the public consciousness, though their importance is mainly in the job application and recruitment phase, whereas keeping the job depends on actual performance as well as on hard-to-measure[6] personality skills, for the enhancement of which some employers actually offer or subsidise e) type programmes.

Except in computing a first-year university student's state grant, no special legal privilege is awarded to those whose diplomas carry the words "with distinction". Employers, however, are likely to give them preference in hiring and/or offer them somewhat higher starting salaries.

4. NATIONAL EQUIVALENCES

Each diploma type a) through d) is valid nationwide under federal law, so that, for example for types a) and (b2), transfer to another school offering the same curriculum is possible at the end of each school year, with a minimum of administrative procedure. Supplementary examinations may be necessary in the civil service when transferring from one employer (federal, local, municipal authority) to another, e.g. in case of differences in provincial law. Generally, partial credit is also given if holders of a certificate desire complementary qualification at the same level in a related field ("horizontal credit").

Provision is also made for official recognition of diplomas between pairs of the above types, particularly if the second type offers an opportunity for upgrading ("vertical credit"). This form of recognition includes:

   – obligatory waiving of theoretical parts of a non-school examination on the basis of certification of school work;

   – recognition of end-of-apprenticeship certificates or master craftsman's diplomas as equivalent to school certificates for admission to higher-level or teacher training programmes (b and c to a);

   – partial credit for full-time vocational school dropouts when transferring to the dual system (a to b);

 – credit for a completed full-time vocational programme in the following forms:

  i) full equivalence to several end-of-apprenticeship examinations (a to b);

  ii) partial credit toward apprenticeship in trades that are only partially related (a to b);

  iii) partial or total waiving of the practical experience required for self-employment (a to c);

  iv) waiving of the master craftsman's examination (proposed; a to c).

While for the purposes of equivalence i) there is a one-to-one relationship between a school-based curriculum and an out-of-school examination, other full-time curricula generally have more breadth but less depth in a given speciality than training under the dual system. Mutual credit is therefore a matter of compromise and must be formally defined for each combination of previous training and desired continuation. This takes the legal form of an ordinance of the federal minister responsible for the continuation: the Minister of Education and Arts for ii) and the Minister of Economic Affairs for iii) and iv), though the other Minister concerned must concur.

Being fairly abstract, the principles of mutual recognition offer considerable leeway to the decision maker. Since "outsiders" seeking recognition have not contributed to the creation or preservation of teaching or training jobs under the "receiving" Ministry's jurisdiction, there is at least sub-conscious pressure toward a tough recognition policy, while the "sending" Ministry will plead for generous equivalences. These equivalences must be renegotiated whenever a new syllabus of the sending Ministry comes into force; until agreement is reached, no equivalences are awarded. In the past this has sometimes meant that desirable curriculum reform has been postponed as long as possible for fear that, because of a tightened recognition policy by the other Ministry, graduates would be worse off than under the old curriculum. Also, whenever previously established equivalences were indeed lost under a new curriculum, both Ministers involved came under sharp public attack.

The solution envisaged in a bill currently before parliament is to abolish equivalences of type i) altogether and substitute type iii) and iv) equivalences. After all, hardly any graduate of a full-time programme is interested in being awarded skilled-worker status, as employers are likely to hire him or her at a higher level in any case. The actual interest is in going into business on his or her own, particularly in the building, commercial, hotel and catering trades and in crafts. Under current law, licences in these trades, even where no master craftsman's examination is prescribed, can only be awarded to holders of germane end-of-apprenticeship diplomas after a minimum period of salaried work. The new bill would cut out this requirement and award licences (and, where applicable, the authority to call oneself a master craftsperson) to graduates of full-time schools as well, thus avoiding the need for end-of-apprenticeship equivalences and the somewhat ludicrous situation where much of the prestige of a programme tended to be measured in terms of the number of end-of-apprenticeship equivalences it carried. In some trades, the new bill would abolish the need for a licence altogether. Still, the new equivalences of types *iii)* and *iv)* would require definition (*e.g.* should a graduate of a gunsmiths' school be allowed to go into business as a balance maker?), and thus renewed contention may be expected.

In the long term, further liberalisation of self-employment may be expected owing to a general change in climate in economic policy and also in assimilation to European Union rules.[7]

5.   INTERNATIONAL EQUIVALENCES

International diversity appears to be much greater in secondary vocational education and training than in the university sphere, where schemes of mutual recognition have a long tradition. Thus, the variety of certificates and diplomas acquired abroad obviously precludes the establishment of formal equivalences for each possible case. Instead, the law provides for individual recognition procedures by the "receiving" Ministry, *i.e.* the Federal Ministry of Education and Arts for certificates of type *a)* or the Federal Ministry of Economic Affairs for certificates of types *b)* and *c)*. There are no international equivalences for civil service purposes (type *d)*. The holder of a foreign document desiring its official recognition must:

- be either an Austrian national or prove residence in Austria;

- submit the relevant certificate(s) and/or diploma(s) (an official translation is required if the language of the document is not German);

- pay an administrative fee.

The first requirement is intended to discourage frivolous applications and to preclude the use of a granted application as an argument in an application for a residency permit.

The application may be:

- granted outright;

- granted on condition that certain supplementary examinations are passed;

- refused.

The decision is based on a comparison of the list of subjects passed and the number of hours each was studied with the relevant Austrian syllabus. If the required information is not discernible in the documents submitted, the applicant is asked to procure further evidence from his school, school authority or embassy.

The majority of applicants are from outside Western Europe. Such applicants are normally enjoined to take supplementary examinations in history and geography, since the subject matter covered by programmes in their own countries differs considerably from the Austrian syllabus. Also, in these cases, if an equivalence is awarded on the basis of school certificates, the concomitant equivalences of type *i*) are not awarded unless the applicant can prove the requisite hours of practical work. Applicants from Western Europe, on the other hand, are not likely to need formal recognition of their certificates and diplomas in the near future, once relevant European Union regulations come into effect.

Austrian vocational certificates and diplomas enjoy a considerable reputation abroad. Yet there is growing concern that, because of the formal structure of the Austrian system of secondary and post-secondary technical schools, deserved equivalence might not be granted to Austrians under European Union regulations. In particular, while graduates of five-year secondary technical programmes in Austria appear to be basically equivalent on the German job market to graduates of German *Fachhochschulen*, they would not be so under EC Guideline 89/48/EWG of 21 December 1988.[8] Certain modifications of the structure of the Austrian school system are therefore under discussion, in particular:

– the creation of an equivalent to the German *Fachhochschulen*;

– improved transfer facilities into full-time education, including university access for graduates of the dual system of training.

6. SYLLABI

Austrian syllabi set out the knowledge and skills to be acquired by students or apprentices in a given curriculum in fairly general terms. The knowledge and skills tested in examinations are precisely those listed in the relevant syllabus.

Detailed specification of a profile of both atomic and compound skills achieved, while theoretically possible, seems less than desirable and is indeed not an issue in Austria. In addition to the disadvantages noted earlier in this paper, a one-off examination of a multiplicity of skills would be subject to numerous statistical errors and thus yield spurious results. Also, Austrian teachers have always enjoyed freedom of method, and too rigid itemisation of subject matter in a syllabus would tend to encroach on this freedom. Finally, a fairly abstract level of specification ensures that syllabi need not be changed with every new advance in technology; since they have the status of ministerial ordinances in Austria, their modification is a time-consuming process.

7. EXAMINERS

Within the school system, examiners are identical with teachers and thus trained at universities or vocational teachers' colleges. Unless their field is general education, they must have had several years' practice in their speciality at the appropriate level; some still hold part-time jobs in business or industry while teaching. They also attend further training programmes from time to time, the average being two to three days per teacher per year.

Federal civil service examiners are appointed by the Federal Chancellor's Office. Usually all but one of them, who is on the staff of the applicant's Ministry, come from that office. Equivalent rules apply at the provincial and municipal levels. Examiners must be top specialists and currently practising in their field; however, no pedagogical training is required.

NOTES

1. It has been suggested in defence of the one-off examination that, rather than gauging the knowledge and skill it purports to test, it measures a candidate's ability to perform under pressure, an aptitude much in demand in today's working world.

2. One important suggestion along these lines is the publication of assessment criteria, such as the weighting of the various answers or components. Though perfect objectiveness is unlikely to be obtainable through such measures, even a slight degree of improvement is highly desirable. Unfortunately it cannot be decreed, but must depend on the willingness and specialised competence of the individual teacher or examiner.

3. These include short technician-level programmes for graduates of secondary general schools (normally grades 13 through 14). Since graduates of these programmes are awarded the same privileges as those of the regular technician-level schools (grades 9 through 13), the former are considered part of the secondary rather than the tertiary system. Three-year colleges of education and of social work are at present the only non-university part of the tertiary sector; they basically embrace the university assessment system, though with some admixtures of type *a*). The lowest university degree is the M.A. or equivalent, awarded after a minimum of eight to ten semesters of study, presentation of a thesis, and formal examinations.

4. Far from being a dead letter, the right to university access is exercised by 44 per cent of technician-level graduates, who, for example, constitute approximately one-third of all freshmen at universities of technology.

5. The resulting collective contracts typically refer to the legally defined levels; they may, however, also recognise programmes of type *e*).

6. Assessment of these skills by a previous employer would constitute a yardstick of sorts, but as the law prohibits negative criticism in testimonials, such an assessment can only be inferred from the documented reason for termination of employment. At any rate, tradition and labour laws have made job changes considerably less common than in Western Europe and North America.

7. After centuries of tight regulation of all trades, it would be too much to expect full liberalisation overnight. There is as yet no national consensus that a person should be allowed to go into business with or without proof of competence. Political practice in Austria would require a consensus of employers' and employees' interest groups for a change in any law having economic repercussions.

8. The problem has recently been alleviated by the passing of EC Guideline 92/51/EWG of 18 June 1992, which regulates the recognition of vocational diplomas awarded after a minimum of one year's post-secondary studies. While the short technician-level programmes mentioned in footnote 3 were originally established as special versions of the secondary technical schools, the tail may henceforth be wagging the dog, since under the wording of the Guideline the declared equivalence of the two types at the national level will ensure recognition of the regular type's diplomas.

CANADA (QUEBEC)

RECOGNITION AND ASSESSMENT
OF THE SKILLS AND COMPETENCES
OF ADULT WORKERS AND OF IMMIGRANTS

by
Claire Prevost-Fournier
Ministry of Education, Quebec

INTRODUCTION

To enable immigrants and individuals educated outside Quebec to practise their profession or pursue their studies based on diplomas or degrees obtained before emigrating, Quebec CEGEPs (*Collèges d'enseignement général et professionnel*) currently employ the process of learning accreditation. Initially developed to assess non-academic learning in order to save individuals from having to duplicate studies for which they already possess equivalences, this system although not perfect is currently the best answer to the immediate needs linked to accrediting prior learning where immigrants are concerned. The current system of accrediting diplomas and degrees obtained abroad establishes equivalences with those issued by the Quebec school system, education equivalences being established by the educational institutions. This paper will describe the process of learning accreditation developed in Quebec, and analyse its relevance in evaluating and accrediting the prior learning of immigrants.

1. THE LEARNING ACCREDITATION PROCESS AS APPLIED IN QUEBEC

One of the first steps in preparing this paper was to identify the goal of learning accreditation, which targets the school system's recognition of an individual's experiential learning to facilitate his or her access to a given profession or programme of studies. The process involves evaluating this learning based on the school system's course and programme objectives. Until recently, the learning evaluated and accredited by the schools was the product of the system in Quebec. Now, this same system is called upon to evaluate prior learning acquired elsewhere, in other environments, such as the labour market, or through socio-cultural activities. In this regard, learning can be defined more specifically as *academic achievement*, *non-academic learning*, or *life experience*. For the purposes of this paper, however, the global term "learning" will be used, which encompasses all possible sources of knowledge acquisition.

What are the foundations of the system and how was it set up? What were the conditions for its implementation in the Quebec education system? What are its inherent problems, and what steps can be taken to solve them? An attempt will be made to answer these questions before discussing the specific application of the learning accreditation process to the case of immigrants.

A brief history of the origins of prior learning accreditation in Quebec

Interestingly enough, the need for a system to accredit prior learning first arose in relation to American soldiers in the post-war years. The United States was forced to develop methods of evaluating and accrediting learning acquired by these individuals as part of their army training or through various other experiences on the labour market and elsewhere specific to the military trade. This accreditation of prior learning targeted both the soldiers' integration into the civilian labour market and their admission into training programmes. A system of evaluating and accrediting the learning acquired by soldiers was set up, and the usefulness of such a system for civilians quickly became obvious.

Based on recommendations of the Commission of Inquiry on Vocational and Socio-Cultural Training for Adults in the early 1980s, the Quebec government decided to supplement its education system with a system of learning accreditation aimed at meeting the specific needs of adults who wanted to return to school or improve their standing on the labour market. In today's advanced industrial society, point-to-point progression through school, leading ultimately to entry into the labour force, is a thing of the past. General and vocational education must be adapted to technological change and market globalisation, while the free flow of goods and people calls for linkage mechanisms between school and the labour market nationally, and between the various education systems internationally. The latter forces people to envisage work/school alternation and professional mobility as unavoidable realities. In this context, learning accreditation is an ideal mechanism for putting continuing education into practice. It also promotes the merging of the world of knowledge acquisition and production with that of the production of goods and services.

Furthermore, since access to qualifying training is, undeniably, one of the objectives of any society, having the education system recognise various sources of knowledge acquisition goes hand in hand with respect for individual rates of progress, thereby making individual training one of the main focuses of educational institutions. The world of knowledge acquisition and production must correspond to the educational, social and cultural aspirations of each individual. This new outlook demands a change in attitude, especially among teaching staff. Teaching and learning evaluation methods must become more diversified to meet the ever-growing needs of both individuals and the labour market.

Implementation and development of the learning accreditation system at the college level

In Quebec, college is the first level of higher or non-compulsory education. It corresponds to the twelfth and thirteenth years of schooling for general education programmes leading to university studies, and to the twelfth, thirteenth and fourteenth years of schooling for vocational education programmes leading directly to the labour market.

Taking individual experience into account when admitting people into secondary, college or university education programmes has been part and parcel of Quebec's school system for many years. The educational institutions, each in their own way, took adults' prior experience into account when admitting them into study programmes. The implementation of a system of learning accreditation served not only to systematise existing practices but also as a guide to learning evaluation.

The Quebec school system's main challenge in implementing the learning accreditation system at the college level was to make it as credible and as widely accepted as the traditional system of learning evaluation, despite the fact that it called for new evaluation approaches. The development of learning accreditation was, therefore, based on school organisation and methods of certification. The study programme became the frame of reference used to accredit learning, with the individual as the focus of the entire process.

During the implementation period, Quebec set up a central agency whose mandate consisted mainly of administering the funds allocated for this project (some C$ 10 million) and informing the educational institutions about the learning accreditation process. These institutions could, on a voluntary basis, submit projects targeting the implementation of learning accreditation services. The central agency played a key role in training the staff of the institutions participating in the implementation process, providing the necessary technical assistance and creating work tools useful in learning evaluation. Disseminating information and conducting studies and research on the project were also among the responsibilities of this agency commissioned to lay the foundations of a system of learning accreditation at the college level.

At present, Quebec is creating maintenance and development mechanisms for learning accreditation for the college network as a whole.

The foundations, functions and principles of learning accreditation

Learning accreditation is based on the following:
- All learning deserves to be recognised *per se*, regardless of where or how it was acquired. The important thing is the content.

- Every individual has the right to show what he or she has learned and have this learning evaluated and accredited by the authorities responsible. This is basic social equity.
- Resource rationalisation requires that individual learning be recognised so that people do not have to pursue studies for which they already possess equivalences.

The process of learning accreditation not only enables individuals to claim credits related to specific courses or programmes, but also helps these people choose the educational or vocational path best suited to them. In this respect, learning accreditation constitutes an educational activity in itself. Furthermore, since showing what you have learned is a compulsory facet of learning accreditation, the process results in a diagnosis which can have positive effects both on the individual in question and on organisations involved in manpower training. During the learning demonstration process, individuals often become aware of the scope of their knowledge, which may in turn motivate them to continue their progression through school and better plan their career. In the same way, the individual's personal profile, once outlined, may become an indicator of manpower training needs for the educational community. Learning accreditation can thus help to efficiently plan manpower development and use its potential to the fullest. These are all functions of the learning accreditation process.

Following the example of the United States, Quebec ensured the stringency and validity of its learning accreditation process by basing its implementation on the following principles:

- That which is credited does not correspond to the experience acquired as such, but rather to the knowledge acquired from this experience.
- The knowledge acquired must be measurable in order to be recognised and credited by an educational institution.
- The learning acquired must be credited solely on the basis of the courses and programmes offered by the institution granting the credits attached thereto.
- The learning must be evaluated by content, measurement and evaluation specialists, who can be recruited from among the teaching staff (Kayembe, 1990, pp. 23-25, 31-32).

Tools for learning accreditation and institutional practices practices

College admission criteria, the definition of programme content, and study certification methods are set out in the Regulation governing the organisation of college studies. The Regulation stipulates that a college "may grant an equivalence where a student shows that he has achieved the objectives of the course for which he is requesting an equivalence, either by previous studies or by out-of-school training. The equivalence does not entitle the student to the credits attached to the course, which does not have to be replaced by another course" (Gouvernement du Québec, 1993, p. 13).

In keeping with the Regulation, learning accreditation involves comparing the learning acquired by each individual with the objectives of each programme course. Given that the Regulation assigns the responsibility for learning evaluation to the educational institutions, it is up to each institution to develop its own learning accreditation system. The Ministry of Education defines the general framework for the content of all programmes leading to the diploma of college studies, but each college must define the specific content of each course in these programmes. Certification of studies is done course by course, based on the credits attributed for the successful achievement of course objectives.

Learning accreditation involves evaluating learning course by course in much the way that learning evaluation is conducted for each course in a given programme. However, since they are used to assess learning from various sources and different eras, the evaluation methods for learning accreditation are necessarily numerous and diverse. Those applying for learning accreditation must have the opportunity to show that they have indeed achieved the objectives linked to the successful completion of each course in a given programme. Consequently, educational institutions must provide these people with the necessary tools. In general, a learning accreditation system should include reception and reference services, guidance services, a measurement and evaluation mechanism, and provision for completing missing credits.

Implementation of the learning accreditation system in Quebec colleges raised the need for methods for evaluating non-academic or experiential learning. This led to the portfolio approach, which included oral and written examinations, and which makes the individual the focus of the learning evaluation process. Compiling a portfolio consists in inventorying and demonstrating each individual's learning in terms of course objectives, for each course for which he or she wishes to be accredited. Once the portfolio has been compiled, the individual is asked to submit it to content, measurement and evaluation specialists for evaluation. The evaluator may insist on a written or oral examination analysing all or part of the individual's overall learning before granting the credits attached to the course in question. In some cases, the individual may have achieved only part of the objectives of the course in question; he or she must then complete the missing credits.

The learning accreditation process thus appears to be a solid foundation for the school system in its attempt to meet the continuing education needs of the labour force. By the same token, learning accreditation, which has the unique educational feature of making the individual the focus of his or her educational or vocational path, seems an ideal means of diversifying the system, not only in its evaluation practices but also in its teaching methods, thus equipping it to meet individual needs. Programmes offered to complete missing credits, in particular, call for the diversification and individualisation of educational methods.

A bank of evaluation tools has been compiled for use in various college courses and, in some cases, technical programmes. These tools are available to all educational institutions. However, the bank is not nearly extensive enough to cover all college courses and programmes. As a result, each educational institution must produce its own evaluation tools for every course for which accreditation is requested. Obviously, this is very expensive for the government, not to mention that criteria vary considerably from one institution to another. As we have seen, the learning accreditation process is valid only if it is based on both measurable knowledge and on a detailed definition of the course objectives. Insofar as the Ministry of Education defines the general framework of the programmes, and the educational institutions do the same for course content, the creation of evaluation tools adapted to each individual context is not a given, and the definition of learning objectives does not necessarily facilitate the accreditation of non-academic learning across the board. The situation is even more complex for so-called compulsory courses linked mainly to the acquisition of basic education.

Problems encountered and possible solutions

Apart from funding, learning accreditation in Quebec currently faces two major obstacles. The first is related to the reference framework for learning recognition, evaluation and accreditation, while the second deals with the programmes offered to complete missing credits.

As already pointed out, the accreditation of non-academic learning requires that the individual show that he or she has successfully achieved the objectives of the course for which he or she wishes to be granted the attached credits. Since the framework for these courses is defined by the government, and the objectives for each course are defined by the institutions themselves and target the acquisition of cognitive knowledge rather than vocational skills, the evaluation of non-academic learning is plagued by a number of obstacles. To what extent can all course objectives be measured immediately? To what extent can knowledge acquired from work experience be measured immediately in terms of a given educational objective? The concern for stringency in learning evaluation during the implementation of the learning accreditation system resulted in the creation of sophisticated evaluation tools, which proved costly. Evaluating people's non-academic learning on a course-by-course basis increases costs further, illustrates the problem of defining course objectives, and highlights the need for uniformity between programme definition and professional qualification standards.

Current programme structure and course-by-course certification of studies make it very difficult to offer programmes which compensate for the credits identified as lacking in each learning accreditation case. Since objectives are defined for each of the courses in a given programme, school organisation is based on course logistics. Educational institutions do not offer parts of courses. Allowing people to take only half of a given course, for example, poses a major challenge to the current organisation of the school system.

However, skills-based programme development has been proposed as a possible solution to problems currently experienced in the learning accreditation process. At the college level, this new method of designing and defining programmes is confirmed with the entry into effect of the Regulation on college studies. It promises a substantial improvement both in educational practices and in their adaptation to the labour market. Since programme development will be based on the acquisition of abilities and skills, it will be easier to identify exactly what is to be evaluated.

Other adjustments in school organisation will be required if the usefulness of the learning accreditation system is to be maximised, for example in the area of certification of studies. Certification could be based on the overall skills and abilities acquired rather than on individual courses. Discussion is currently under way on this proposal. Clearly, skills-based programme development could be the solution to a number of problems.

2. LEARNING ACCREDITATION FOR IMMIGRANTS: A CASE IN POINT

The social and vocational integration of immigrants has long been one of Quebec's priorities and continues to be so, judging by the recent position taken by the Quebec Government. The *ministère des Communautés culturelles et de l'Immigration* recently published a policy statement and a plan of action on immigration and the integration of immigrants. These documents encourage the MCCI's partners to work together to ensure that immigrants receive the reception and services to which they are entitled, so that they can integrate harmoniously into the society they have chosen to enter. The learning accreditation services offered by colleges reflect this desire to integrate immigrants into Quebec society, based on their educational and vocational potential.

Accreditation of titles, degrees and diplomas

For some 30 years now, Quebec has been equipped to accredit and validate professional titles, degrees and diplomas obtained by those educated abroad and, consequently, by immigrants. To do so, attestations of equivalences are issued indicating the Quebec education level corresponding to studies completed abroad. These attestations serve to situate people on the labour market and indicate to educational institutions the education level completed. Professional corporations governing the practice of exclusive professions or those with reserved titles must, under Quebec's Professional Code, establish equivalence standards for foreign diplomas and degrees to make these professions accessible to immigrants.

To define the standards used to evaluate the files submitted to it, Quebec uses documents produced by international organisations such as UNESCO, the OECD, etc. It also refers to multilateral agreements, such as the UNESCO Convention on the Recognition of Studies, Diplomas and Degrees in Higher Education in the States of the region of Europe and North America, and to bilateral agreements on university degrees and admission criteria signed between Quebec and various countries such as Cameroon, Belgium and France. Quebec has also produced an equivalence guide which is updated annually with new titles and data on various foreign education systems.

Accreditation of learning

To meet the challenge posed by Quebec's multi-ethnic reality, the reception and integration of immigrants and ethnic groups has been the object of research and action at the college level for many years. Despite these efforts, evaluating and accrediting learning acquired by immigrants remains a complex, delicate operation.

An attestation of equivalence issued to immigrants indicates a level of education completed abroad in terms of Quebec's education system. As mentioned above, it does not constitute an evaluation of the learning content. The relevance of the learning acquired as compared to Quebec study programmes remains to be shown. This means that immigrants must submit an application to educational institutions to have their learning evaluated based on the content of their programmes.

Given the difficulty of obtaining the description of courses taken abroad and the documents attesting to the person's level of schooling, it is often impossible for educational institutions to attribute course equivalences. In such cases, the applications are processed using learning accreditation services.

The educational institutions ask immigrants to compile a portfolio showing what they have learned. In Quebec, the focus is on academic rather than non-academic learning. Although learning accreditation seems the process most likely to enable immigrants to demonstrate their academic learning based on the objectives of Quebec study programmes, a number of obstacles crop up when it is applied.

First, compiling a portfolio requires a certain mastery of the language of the country of adoption. Immigrants are at a disadvantage, since they must describe and demonstrate their learning in a language of which they often possess only the rudiments. A possible solution to this problem would be for the educational institutions to offer refresher courses in French before admitting immigrants into any programme. Second, the cultural background of immigrants influences their attitude toward demonstrating their learning and also determines the essence of what they have learned. Transposing this learning to the Quebec educational context is a challenge in itself. As a partial solution to this problem, which is specific to immigrants, a course on compiling a portfolio has been set up for these individuals.

Cultural differences also affect the way each person's learning is evaluated, not to mention the definition of the evaluation references and criteria themselves. To remedy this, training sessions will be set up, not only for immigrants but also for all those involved in evaluating their learning, from those working in reception and reference services to the actual evaluator.

The practice of a profession in a social, cultural, economic and political environment calls for certain adjustments. The development of programmes offered to complete missing credits should enable people to acquire knowledge of the standards and values pertaining to the practice of said profession in Quebec.

The use of the learning accreditation process does not ensure that studies completed abroad will automatically be considered in the educational and vocational integration of immigrants; as indicated, a number of problems remain to be solved. However, at the college level, research is currently being conducted to better identify the learning accreditation needs of immigrants, thereby promoting – in keeping with the foundations and principles of the learning accreditation process – the development of permanent solutions with a view to ensuring immigrants' fully fledged integration into schools and the labour market based on each individual's potential.

BIBLIOGRAPHY

BERTHELOT, J. (1991), *Apprendre à vivre ensemble : immigration, société et éducation*, 2nd ed., Editions Albert Saint-Martin, Montreal.

BIRON, J., CARETTE, J. and VERREAULT, C. (1990), *Vocabulaire de l'éducation*, 2nd ed., Les Publications du Québec, Quebec City.

Comité mixte en reconnaissance des acquis extrascolaires au collégial (1992*a*), *La reconnaissance des acquis au collégial : Bulletin d'information*, Vol. I, No. I, Montreal, January-February.

Comité mixte en reconnaisance des acquis extrascolaires au collégial (1992*b*), *La reconnaissance des acquis au collégial : Bulletin d'information*, Vol. I, No. 2, Montreal, May-June.

Conseil des collèges (1992*a*), *L'éducation des adultes dans le CEGEP : rapport sur l'état et les besoins de l'enseignement collégial*, Gouvernement du Québec, Quebec City, March.

Conseil des collèges (1992*b*), *L'enseignement collégial : des priorités pour un renouveau de la formation. Rapport sur l'état et les besoins de l'enseignement collégial*, Gouvernement du Québec, Quebec City.

Conseil supérieur de l'éducation (1992*a*), *Accroître l'accessibilité et garantir l'adaptation : l'éducation des adultes dix ans après la Commission Jean. Avis au ministre de l'Education et au ministre de l'Enseignement supérieur et de la Science*, Quebec City.

Conseil supérieur de l'éducation (1992*b*), *Une formation accessible et adaptée : qu'en pensent les adultes et le personnel. Rapport d'une recherche menée en éducation des adultes auprès des étudiantes et des étudiants et du personnel du secondaire, du collégial et de l'universitaire*, Turcotte, C., assisted by S. Fontaine and P.-H. Lamontagne, Quebec City.

DESLAURIERS, J.-P. (1991), *La recherche qualitative : Guide pratique*, McGraw-Hill Editeurs, Montreal.

Direction de la classification des enseignants (1992), *Le guide d'attribution d'équivalence*, ministère de l'Éducation, Gouvernement du Québec, Quebec City.

Direction des communications (1991), *Au Québec pour bâtir ensemble : Plan d'action gouvernemental en matière d'immigration et d'intégration*, ministère des Communautés culturelles et de l'Immigration, Gouvernement du Québec, Quebec City.

Direction des politiques et programmes (1990), *Au Québec pour bâtir ensemble : Énoncé de politique en matière d'immigration et d'intégration*, ministère des Communautés culturelles et de l'Immigration, Gouvernement du Québec, Quebec City.

Direction générale de l'enseignement collégial (1989), *La reconnaissance des acquis au collégial : Des orientations à privilégier pour la Direction générale de l'enseignement collégial*, Direction générale de l'enseignement collégial, Quebec City, February.

Direction générale de l'enseignement collégial (1990), *Circuit collégial 1990-1991*, ministère de l'Enseignement supérieur et de la Science, Gouvernement du Québec, Quebec City.

Editeur officiel du Québec (1991), *Code des professions : Lois refondues du Québec*, chapitre C-26 à jour au 5 février 1991, Editeur officiel du Québec, Quebec City.

Fédération des CEGEPS (1991), *Mémoire sur l'éducation des adultes présenté au ministre de l'Enseignement supérieur et de la Science*, Montreal.

FONTAINE, P. (1991), *Accueil et intégration des personnes issues des minorités ethniques au collégial: Inventaire des mesures et des besoins exprimés dans les CEGEPS anglophones*, Direction générale de l'enseignement collégial, ministère de l'Enseignement supérieur et de la Science, Gouvernement du Québec, Quebec City, January.

Gouvernement du Québec (1984), *Un projet d'éducation permanente : Énoncé d'orientation et plan d'action en éducation des adultes*, Gouvernement du Québec, Quebec.

Gouvernement du Québec (1993), *Colleges Education Regulations*.

Groupe de travail interministériel sur la reconnaissance des acquis (1987), *Rapport du Groupe de travail interministériel sur la reconnaissance des acquis au Comité interministériel de l'éducation des adultes*, October.

KAYEMBE, N.-B. (1990), *La reconnaissance des acquis au collégial : Bientôt six ans. Rapport d'évaluation*, Fédération des CEGEP, Montreal, January.

LAMONTAGNE, J. (1990), *État de ce que fait le ministère de l'Éducation en terme de reconnaissance des diplômes acquis à l'étranger*, ministère de l'Education du Québec, Direction de la classification des enseignants, Quebec City, October.

LECLERC, C. (1990), *La présence des minorités linguistiques au collégial*, Direction générale de l'enseignement collégial, ministère de l'Enseignement supérieur et de la Science, Gouvernement du Québec, Quebec City, November.

LECLERC, C. (1991), "La présence des minorités linguistiques au collégial", *Pédagogie collégiale*, Vol. 4, No. 4, Montreal, May.

LEMAY, D. (1990), *Accueil et intégration des personnes issues des minorités ethniques au collégial: inventaire des mesures et des besoins exprimés dans les CEGEPS francophones*, Direction générale de l'enseignement collégial, ministère de l'Enseignement supérieur et de la Science, Gouvernement du Québec, Quebec City, Autumn.

LEMAY, D. (1991), "L'accueil et l'intégration des étudiantes et des étudiants des minorités ethniques dans les CEGEPS de langue française", *Pédagogie collégiale*, Vol. 4, No. 4, Montreal, May.

Ministère de l'Enseignement supérieur et de la Science (1991), *Recherche-action sur la reconnaissance des acquis au collégial à l'intention des clientèles ethniques et des personnes immigrantes : Projet présenté au Fonds d'initiatives pour le soutien de projets favorisant l'intégration*, August.

Ministère de l'Enseignement supérieur et de la Science (1992), *Projet d'élaboration d'un plan d'intervention systémique pour la reconnaissance des acquis au collégial à l'intention des personnes immigrantes : Projet présenté au Fonds d'initiatives pour le soutien de projets favorisant l'intégration*, March.

FRANCE

EXAMINATIONS IN A CENTRALISED, SCHOOL-BASED TRAINING SYSTEM

by
Benoît Bouyx
Directorate of *Lycées* and Colleges, Ministry of Education, Paris

Although in general education terms examinations are essentially passports to further study, in vocational programmes they are primarily intended to give access to the labour market and to recognise individual qualifications. The French vocational examination system is distinguished by its national scope: diplomas are valid nationwide and include a statement of examination content. The nationwide validity of diplomas, which has evolved over time, has the two great advantages of fostering individual mobility and of ensuring that the various occupations will recognise and endorse the diplomas (particularly through collective agreements). On the debit side, the system is accused of being rigid and insensitive to local realities, and of overemphasizing the academic aspect of knowledge and know-how. In what follows, the current examination system, with the changes made over the last few years or now under way, will be described.

1. THE TRADITIONAL SYSTEM AND ITS LIMITATIONS

The main feature of the French system is that many kinds of candidates may take a given examination: school children, apprentices, adults, and other individual candidates, all of whom may sit the same examination provided they meet the entry conditions.

Examinations are set, just as diplomas are granted, at the national level: the number, kind and weighting of tests as well as their definitions are all prescribed. In general, tests fall into two categories: general tests and technological or vocational ones, the proportion of each depending on the type of diploma (scientific tests have in most cases traditionally been included in the general part).

Examinations take place at the level of one or more academies (school districts). They are marked by boards that are generally tripartite (employers, wage-earners, teachers) and must be chaired by an employer, for certain diplomas, and by inspectorate representatives for others. The tests may be written, practical or oral.

They sometimes take the form of a board interview following the preparation of a file or probationary period report.

A few months before the examinations, the inspectors who are to organise them have subjects prepared by teachers. They then convene subject selection committees, made up of professionals, which choose the subject to be set. All candidates sit the examinations at the same place, and professionals attend the practical tests. Once the tests have been completed and corrected, the board meets to reach a final decision.

The way examinations now work is open to a number of criticisms: because they are "one-off", good or bad luck plays too great a role (one may be in good or poor form on the day of the test, a question one has reviewed recently may or may not come up, etc.) and, because they are academic and artificial, they do not show how people would fare in an actual work situation.

For example, to gauge a mason's abilities, he is asked to build a false wall (involving a set of difficulties he will never meet with on the job), out of false concrete (since the wall will have to be demolished after the examination), in a false work situation (since each candidate builds his wall alone, whereas his working life will most often be spent as part of a team)!

A third criticism levelled against examinations is that they are "make or break". Over the last few years, several attempts have been made to change this:

- In one approach, checks on progress are made progressive through the introduction of continuous assessment and assessment during training.
- A second approach is to allow diplomas to be earned in stages on a cumulative credit basis.

2. RECENT CHANGES

An experiment was launched in 1972 in 12 vocational *lycées* whereby knowledge would be continuously assessed and no final examination would be held. The goal was to replace the examination grind, which must result in failure for many pupils, by a pattern of success, as the pupil added to his store of knowledge at his own pace. If he did not achieve the desired result within the normal period of schooling, he would be able to opt for various forms of extension.

This experiment also gave rise to the design of benchmark-type diplomas, for if it was to act as a progressive, incremental check on knowledge gained, the diploma had to be defined not in terms of curricula and examination tests, but in terms of ultimate objectives which could be broken down into intermediate objectives.

Following the decision to extend this approach progressively to all entry-level diplomas, another approach was taken when the vocational *baccalauréat* was created: assessment during training. Experience had shown that continuous assessment, though a very attractive approach to checking acquired knowledge, was extremely demanding and difficult to apply widely.

When the vocational *baccalauréat* was created, therefore, a middle course was taken. As mandatory periods of on-the-job training were introduced and it was desired to take these into account at examination time, new ways of doing so had to be found.

On-the-job training had been made mandatory in recognition of the training capacity of business, and the fact that certain skills can only be acquired on the job. This is particularly true of all those skills linked to real work situations, which are assessed by the pupil's tutor in co-operation with the trainer. The examination leading to the vocational *baccalauréat* is therefore structured as seven tests, of which three are based on assessment during training.

What is meant by this? One-time final tests, which normally took place in June of each year, are replaced by "evaluation situations" spread out over the term of the training and organised by the teaching team itself. The situation in which the teacher had no role in the process of certification of his pupils has been totally reversed: it is now the teacher's responsibility to verify that the objectives laid down in the diploma for each evaluation situation have been achieved.

This new approach has important advantages: it introduces a progressive verification of knowledge acquired, it is more sensitive to actual educational situations, and it de-emphasizes the examination. This system, which originated with the creation of the vocational *baccalauréat*, has been progressively extended to all entry-level vocational training.

3. FACILITATING THE CERTIFICATION AND VALIDATION OFCOMPETENCES

For more than 20 years now, in order to help adults achieve certification, an experiment has been going on whereby diplomas are issued on the basis of credits that can be accumulated. The diplomas are broken down into fields (for instance a vocational field, a French language field, a maths and science field, and a current events field), each of these fields being further broken down into several credits.

Each credit can be taken in either of two ways:

– under continuous assessment;

– through testing.

For a long time, only continuous assessment was used. It proved to be a remarkable tool for the process of qualifying blue-collar workers that was undertaken by some large companies. However, the results were more notable for their quality than their quantity, as until the 1990s the number of diplomas granted under this procedure remained small.

A new approach subsequently began to be taken whereby periodic tests were administered by special centres so that any adult who wished to have his skills recognised by a state diploma could find places open at any time of the year where he could obtain all or part of a diploma. Significantly more diplomas were granted on a cumulative credit basis under this system.

This way of granting diplomas, which in the beginning had been exclusively reserved for adults, was extended to entry-level training for schoolchildren and apprentices in 1993.

In 1994, after some 20 years of experience with this system and in view of the strong demand for diplomas it generated, consideration was given to ways of improving its operation and its consistency.

More changes are taking place with the implementation of an Act on recognition of occupational skills promulgated in 1992. The Act makes it mandatory for diploma-granting bodies to recognise occupational skills of persons with five years of job experience by exempting them from testing of skills acquired during their working life. The implementation of the Act poses a real challenge to the education system, which must equip itself to respond to an ever-increasing demand.

Another powerful effect of the Act, however, is to encourage the transition from a system of examinations that rewards academic knowledge and ways of learning that do not reflect job experience, to a system that rewards skills that may have been acquired without any formal education.

The goals to be attained are: recognition of acquired skills by analysis of job experience rather than examination tests; and exemption, on the strength of these acquired skills, from testing of even general academic subjects! Those in charge of testing must therefore re-think their approach completely: they can no longer simply design tests and administer them to candidates, but now have to assess skills actually acquired by analysing employment histories.

Official recognition of occupational skills therefore raises the problem of the "meaning" of occupational examinations. Are they to act as a check on academic knowledge or on skills pertinent to actual work situations?

France has a long tradition of examinations, the *baccalauréat* examinations being the model for the rest. This system can, at least in theory, establish an average performance profile, but when it comes to gauging ability to do a particular job, it has serious shortcomings. The occupational skills certification system will inevitably have to distance itself more and more from the system now used for general education in order to maintain its credibility, and act as a true passport to employment and the recognition of individual qualifications.

GERMANY

THE INSTITUTIONAL FRAMEWORK
AND CERTIFICATION IN THE DUAL SYSTEM

by
Wilfried Reisse
Federal Institute for Vocational Training, Berlin

1. THE CHALLENGE OF LINKING THE EDUCATIONAL SYSTEM AND THE EMPLOYMENT SYSTEM

Connecting the education system and the employment system is a very difficult but important task. One approach is the so-called "dual system" of vocational training in Germany. Assessment for certification and instructional assessment are key elements of this system.

Assessment of initial vocational training in Germany is based on a uniform national system defined by the Vocational Training Act. In this system, national goals and objectives in vocational training are assessed for certification and licence. By means of a "triple certification system", each student receives three different certificates at the end of his vocational training programme: a certificate based on an examination, a certificate delivered by the employer (a type of employment record), and a vocational college report.

The most important certificate for assessing national goals and objectives in vocational training is the examination-based certificate, supplemented by the two other certificates. This paper describes the legal base, the structure (written, practical and sometimes oral examinations), the content and the procedures for the examinations.

This system of assessment in vocational training, in particular through a common final examination, offers important benefits: a uniform level of vocational qualifications in the labour force is maintained and controlled; employers obtain valid information for hiring employees; the uniform qualification level is a reference for negotiating wages; students are strongly motivated for vocational training because of the advantages of possessing certificates; and implementation of new training regulations is strongly supported.

But there are still some unsolved problems: the balance between the three certificates is a matter of discussion (the relation between external assessment by

unified examinations and internal assessment of students); higher-level competences are difficult to measure; and financing the assessment system seems
expensive.

Vocational examinations and instructional assessment are included as a sub-
system (system of vocational assessment) of the training system. At best, such
assessments and the corresponding certificates may function as a kind of link
between these two systems.

2. THE DUAL SYSTEM OF VOCATIONAL TRAINING

The most important type of initial vocational training in Germany is, by far, a
special system of co-operation between companies and vocational schools (the so-
called "dual" system), based on the Vocational Training Act (*Berufsbildungsgesetz*)
of 1969. Among the basic elements of the dual system:

- It is termed "dual" because all students receive training at two sites, namely
  in their firm and in part-time vocational colleges. Most of the training (usually three/four days a week) takes place in-house. The training programme
  generally takes three years to complete.

- The legal foundation for training is different for each place of learning (the
  federal government is responsible for the regulation of company training,
  and the different *Länder* for school-based training). The in-house part of the
  training is based on uniform regulations issued by the federal government,
  in accordance with the Vocational Training Act.

- The system is also called "dual" because governmental organisations and
  the economic system co-operate in providing education.

The dual system is not limited to traditional apprenticeships in the crafts
trades but covers 380 "federally recognised occupations" in trade and administration, industry, services, agriculture, health, etc.

The following statistics provide a better picture:

- In the past ten years, more than 70 per cent of individuals in each age group
  were trainees in one of the recognised training jobs. Therefore, examinations
  in vocational training are the most common examinations in Germany.

- In 1988 nearly 1.5 million students were tested in different examinations
  based on the Vocational Training Act.

- The passing rate in the final examinations varies between 85-95 per cent.

3. ASSESSMENT IN THE DUAL SYSTEM

Quite a diversity of examinations and evaluations exist in the area of vocational training: entrance examinations including tests and interviews conducted by

firms, assessments of aptitude during the probationary period in the company, class tests, other kinds of achievement evaluations and appraisals as well as mid-term reports in vocational school, regular evaluation of on-the-job performance and/or behaviour, assessment in courses held in interplant training institutions, intermediate examinations, performance evaluations when applying for early admission to the final or journeyman's examinations, "practice tests" before the final examination, evaluations and examinations in connection with the three final certificates (examination-based, training employer, vocational college), other company-specific examinations held at the end of training, and appraisals concerning suitability for continued employment once training has ended.

The Vocational Education Act, which contains the legal regulations governing vocational training in the dual system, defines over 25 different types of examinations, evaluations and performance assessment. The spectrum of educational assessment can be differentiated according to the following:

- *scope and type of legal requirements* for such examinations (for example, there are hardly any regulations concerning entrance examinations for trainees, but quite detailed requirements for final examinations and journeyman's examinations);
- *objectives and functions* of such assessments (final certification or educational assessment);
- *methods* which are applied in this process (tests and examinations assessing the present level of achievement administered at specific points in time, or continuous, long-term observation and evaluation).

The most interesting of these types of assessment is the final assessment for certification at the end of initial vocational training.

4. THE TRIPLE CERTIFICATION SYSTEM CONCLUDING INITIAL VOCATIONAL TRAINING

Every trainee receives three certificates at the end of vocational training: an examination-based certificate, a training employer certificate as a type of employment record, and a vocational college report (see Schmidt and Reisse, 1983, pp. 181-201):

- the *examination certificate*: a report of the state-wide final examination administered to all examinees regardless of their locality of training (also called skilled craftsman assistant certificate, or business or commercial assistant certificate);
- the *training employer certificate*: a certificate issued by the instructor or company of training (apprenticeship certificate); and

– the *vocational college report*: a certificate also issued by the specific site of instruction.

Because these certificates are interdependent they are viewed as components of a "triple certification system".

The examination certificate

Since this is the most important certificate for assessing national goals and objectives in vocational training, it will be the focus of analysis in the following section.

A state-wide "standardised certificate", the examination certificate, is issued by the responsible authorities (for example, chamber of trades, or chamber of industry and commerce) on the basis of a final examination. Both training firm and vocational school are supposed to participate in the administration of this examination. The examination itself and the report, not to mention the entire course of training, are oriented toward the achievement of specific minimum requirements as laid down by the training regulations and core curriculum. To describe this assessment and certification system in detail it is necessary to define the components of the system.

Results

Certificates and their features constitute the first component: the results of the system.

Goals and objectives

The content or the behaviour (objectives) to be assessed constitutes another component of the system. Here the concept of "uniform minimum competence testing" is essential.

The goals and objectives of assessment in initial vocational training in Germany are based primarily on a uniform system at the national level supported by the Vocational Training Act. Examination standards are specified in national training regulations. Through these goals and objectives in vocational training a standardised minimum level of competence is prescribed. There is enough leeway so that examination contents can be adapted to new technological developments.

Most important are those goals and objectives on a national level which are relevant to a number of training occupations. For example:

- National law states that the term "vocational training" denotes a very broad type of training and includes some theoretical courses (such as the sciences). This principle has a strong impact on the examination content.
- The discipline "Economics and politics" is relevant for all trainees; other subjects are for technical occupations in particular.
- Higher-level competences, which are relevant for all or a group of training occupations strongly influence examination content. Such competences are also called "key qualifications" or "transferable skills".

The answer to the question "Which contents are the subject of the examination?" is more complex than expected at first sight. There is no list of concrete questions to be asked. The content of each examination must first be researched and described in detail. The implementation of official guidelines for examination requirements of specific questions requires much time and energy. The starting point is a broad definition of the subject to be covered by the examination, including every potential test item. This encompasses the basic training regulation and the "material presented in vocational school instruction, relevant for training in that occupation" (*Berufsbildungsgesetz*, 1969, §35). It is generally assumed that the contents of instruction are composed of those elements in the state-wide standardised basic curriculum for vocational schools which correspond largely to the basic training curriculum for companies. Since this entire body of knowledge cannot be tested largely in the exam, those contents which seem especially important are explicitly stated in the examination requirements; nevertheless, other contents are not excluded.

Procedures and instruments

The examination structure for the final examination in German vocational training is rather simple. In practical examinations two different methods are used:

- examination tasks (or products);
- work sample tests.

In the first case, only the result of the practical task is scored, such as a part of a machine produced during the examination (product-oriented assessment). In work sample tests, the procedure the examinee uses is also of interest, for example in trouble-shooting tasks (process-oriented assessment). In written examinations, objective tests are often used. In recent years there has been a growing interest in short-answer or essay testing. Oral examinations are not administered very often. They are used sometimes as a complement in critical cases, where students may fail the examination in spite of good appraisals of prior training in school or in the training company. Strategies for using the information for decision-making are also part of this system component.

The examination procedure is comprised of the following main elements:

- *Structure of the examination*

A relatively simple structure is described in the recommendation issued in 1980 by the executive committee of the Federal Institute for Vocational Training ("Standardisation Recommendation"). The following components are defined for industrial occupations:

- skill tests including test pieces and/or work samples;

- knowledge tests covering four standard examination subjects (technology, technical mathematics, draughtsmanship, economics and social studies), which may be subdivided into examination areas.

For commercial-administrative occupations, the examination is divided into examination subjects (the regulation does not state which subjects must be tested nor their number) and examination areas. The subject "practical exercises" is often included.

In more recent training regulations this rather rigid scheme has been interpreted more flexibly, and this trend, which seems to be continuing, should be welcomed. For example, the revised regulations for vocational training in the field of metal and electronics contain a new mandatory examination subject, "work planning", which covers general qualifications from other subjects and parts of the examination.

- *Examination methods*

Usually a distinction is made between methods for the written and for the practical examination. In written examinations free-response questions and multiple-choice questions are used. Oral examinations are mandatory only in a few occupations. However, almost all regulations provide for oral exams in addition to the regular examinations. They may be carried out in cases in which the individual has a chance to pass the examination if he/she performs well orally.

Reference should be made to a regulation which is only applied when the training regulations do not mention oral examinations. In this case, the examining board can decide on an oral examination "if the trainee's performance in vocational school or at the training site differs considerably from the examination results up to that point" (*Bundesausschu*, 1971, Vol. 10, *cf.* §13, 3*b*: "Model examination regulation"). This is probably the only instance in which previous achievements can have an indirect influence on a final examination.

Another type of oral examination concerns "practical exercises" for commercial and business trainees who "shall be tested in the form of an interview" (*Hauptausschu*, 1980, §13).

- *Grading procedures*

A grid consisting of 100 points, permitting the conversion of points into grades, plays an important role (*Bundesausschu*, 1971, Vol. 10, *cf.* §20, "Model examination regulation"). The distinctions between levels are not even (for example: 92-100 points = grade 1 [excellent], 30-49 points = grade 5 [poor], 0-29 points = 6 [fail]).

- *Decision-making procedures*

The conditions for passing the examination are formulated in precise and narrow terms in the regulations (*Berufsbildungsgesetz*, 1969, §39-40), and are the same for all training occupations. The criteria for deciding under which circumstances the examination results count as passing are not always uniformly defined in the examination requirements. The standardisation recommendation (*Hauptausschu*, 1980) provides the basis for decision-making in this case. For example, in industrial occupations the trainee must have attained at least an average of grade 4 "satisfactory" in both the skill exam and in the knowledge exam, as well as in the subject "technology" of the knowledge exam. In commercial-administrative occupations this is required for the total grade (average), as well as for certain subjects (so-called "key subjects"). In addition, the candidate fails the examination if he obtains a fail grade in any single subject.

Trainees/students (examinees)

All too often, one tends to forget the persons who are most strongly affected by assessment: the examinees or, in a broader sense, the trainees or students.

Infrastructure

The conditions and prerequisites for implementing and operating the assessment system constitute the infrastructure of the system. The large number of final and journeyman's examinations which are conducted every year could not be handled if the necessary infrastructure did not exist. The following are components of the infrastructure:

- *Financing*

The examinations are primarily financed by the companies in industry and commerce providing the training. The federal government only contributes by providing teacher representatives free of charge to participate in examination boards. Since examinations can be quite expensive, it is justified to calculate costs and benefits. A relevant question in this regard is whether it is possible to keep the expenses of examinations within reasonable limits without reducing their quality and validity.

- *Organisation*

Examinations can be organised in different ways. Often, the co-operation between the "responsible authority" (in the trades, the guilds usually play the role of the chamber of commerce) and the examination boards is supported by special committees of institutions which prepare questions for the national-level examinations. In the guidelines of the Federal Committee for Vocational Training, preference is given to such standardised question sets: the examination boards are "requested" to give priority to such questions (*Bundesausschu*, 1971, Vol. 10, §14, Section 2, "Model examination regulation").

- *Examiners*

The qualifications of those who prepare, administer and mark examinations (and especially of the members of examination boards) are crucial in ensuring the quality of the examinations.

An adequate infrastructure is a prerequisite for conducting comparable examinations. It is not necessary to emphasize the importance of finding competent examiners – a document published by the main committee (*Hauptausschu*, 1991) illustrates that conducting examinations is a demanding task requiring special qualifications.

The legal foundations

In Germany, examinations in vocational training are based on a federal law which provides regulations for certain details of the other components. They are also based on recommendations issued by federal committees.

The specifications for final and journeyman's examinations are relatively detailed. These exams are based on the provisions of the Vocational Education Act as well as the trade regulations. The following specifications are important:

- the examination requirements in the respective training regulation, which define the contents;

- the examination regulations of the responsible authorities, which focus more on the examination procedures.

In order to achieve a certain degree of uniformity of examinations in different training occupations and in different geographical regions, two mechanisms exist:

- Examination requirements are based on the "Recommendation for the Standardisation of Examination Requirements in Training Regulations".

– The examination regulations of the responsible authorities are based on the "Guidelines of the Federal Committee for Vocational Training 1971" (which include the "model examination regulation" – see *Bundesausschu*, 1971).

Reference should also be made to recommendations by the courts. These legal prescriptions are supplemented by a series of recommendations issued by the Federal Committee for Vocational Training and the present Main Committee of the Federal Institute for Vocational Training, which are concerned with the assessment of learning outcomes, and the conduct of assessments and examinations:

– intermediate examinations;

– oral examinations;

– consideration of the special needs of the handicapped in intermediate, final and journeyman's examinations;

– "programmed" examinations (objective written testing);

– qualifications of examination staff.

The examiner is made aware that these detailed regulations prohibit him/her from acting as a kind of independent judge examining according to personal criteria. Instead, the examiner has the function of an expert who applies regulations and recommendations.

The training employer certificate

The training employer certificate provides supplementary information since it is based on long-term observation and evaluation, as well as on other methods for assessing trainee progress during the entire training period. A special version exists which can be issued upon request of the trainee. This more detailed report provides information on conduct, performance and special abilities, and encompasses much more than the standard examination report. It reflects the individual features of the training organisation. Section 8 of the BBiG (Vocational Training Act) provides the lawful foundation for issuing this certificate. From a legal viewpoint, it may be considered a type of employer reference.

The vocational college report

The vocational school report, another locally issued certificate, is based on continuous assessment of student achievement (in contrast to the examination report, but similar to the training report) in vocational school classes. The school law of each state lays down the particulars regarding this certificate. It is a typical school report which differs considerably from the training certificate as to its legal basis and form.

A mixed approach to assessment and certification

This system is a mixture of external and internal assessment. Some disadvantages of external assessment (Macintosh, 1990, pp. 502-504; Kreeft, 1991, pp. 101-110) may be avoided by this combination.

Final and journeyman's examinations as the basis of the examination certificate are a form of "external performance evaluation". Examination systems are termed "external" when the examinations are administered by persons or institutions outside of the school or learning setting and the examiners have no connection to the examinees. An external evaluation corresponds to the principle: teachers are not allowed to be examiners.

The training employer certificate and the vocational college report are both examples of internal performance evaluation and correspond to the principle: teachers and trainers may also evaluate.

These three certificates are linked to one another and comprise a kind of "certification system" for vocational education although they have developed independently and are not co-ordinated. There are good reasons for assuming that the certificates complement each other to a certain degree so that one can view them as different indicators of occupational competence (Schmidt and Reisse, 1983, pp. 181-201). In addition, this approach, implementing three different methods which are almost independent of one another for evaluating trainees, reduces the risk of making incorrect evaluations and placing trainees at a disadvantage.

The real question is to find out which of the three certificates is appropriate for assessing which qualifications using which evaluation and examination methods. One must accept the fact that some important qualifications cannot be assessed directly at all and therefore cannot be certified; at best, they can only be inferred from other characteristics of the person.

In the scope of this paper, it is not possible to deal with the question of whether the system of three certificates is a balanced one. The significance of assessments of trainees by the training firms in connection with these three certificates is discussed in more detail in Reisse (1992, pp. 419-440).

5.   THE ROLE OF PRESSURE GROUPS

Training and assessment are strongly influenced by powerful pressure groups and organisations in Germany. These pressure groups are an important part of the vocational training system and also of the assessment and certification subsystem. The following groups strongly influence all decisions concerning vocational training, for example setting goals and standards:

- employer associations;
- trade unions;

– federal government;

– government of the *Länder*.

Representatives of these organisations constitute the main committee of the Federal Institute for Vocational Training.

6. THE ROLE OF THE CERTIFICATION SYSTEM IN TRAINING AND IN THE LABOUR MARKET: BENEFITS AND PROBLEMS

Objectives and limitations of the examination certificate

To describe the role of the certification system in training and the labour market, it seems useful to start with the legally defined objective of the examination certificate as the most important of the three final certificates concluding initial vocational training.

"The purpose of the final examination is to determine if the examinee possesses the required skills, has acquired the necessary practical and theoretical knowledge, and is familiar with those contents of vocational school instruction which are relevant for learning the occupation. The training regulations must be taken into account" (*Berufsbildungsgesetz*, 1969, §35).

In accordance with legal provisions, the examination report can be characterised by the following features (Reisse, 1989, pp. 193-198):

– Final examinations are the sole basis for decision-making.

– There is an orientation toward minimal requirements.

– There is an orientation toward standardised nationwide requirements.

– The learning sites, namely school and firm, have an obligation to co-operate.

– It is sufficient to make a decision between passing/failing.

– Assessment focuses solely on the student's performance, not his personality.

On the basis of these characteristics, it is possible to define the functions a final or journeyman's examination can and should have. The examinations do not fill the following functions:

– certify performance exceeding minimal requirements;

– have goals of selection (continued employment after training);

– assess the learning process or promote it;

– assess and check the outcomes of training by the firm and the school, and by individual trainers or teachers.

By defining the functions of final and journeyman's examinations so narrowly, unrealistic expectations are avoided and attainable goals can be focused on. In addition, it becomes clear which functions are potentially open for the other two certificates. Nevertheless, sometimes the final examination and the exam certificate play a role that they should not.

The high estimation of the examination report is due to the fact that specific entitlements are linked to it or that the bearer of the certificate has certain advantages. Some of these benefits are established by legislation and jurisdiction, such as admittance to advanced training courses requiring graduation from basic vocational training; as a prerequisite for entitlement to certain wage rates, advantages in the case of unemployment, disability, and for pension claims (Benner, 1977, pp. 20-25).

In general, the impact of the triple certification system on the labour market seems to be very complex – a field of future research. For example, to be admitted to one job it may be sufficient to possess an examination certificate, while for other jobs this may be a necessary but insufficient condition, and a training employer certificate from a well-recognised company may be also necessary. The examination certificate is always linked to a certain wage level – but not with a guarantee of a job. The certificates concluding initial vocational training are neither entitlements nor licences for a position in the labour market – they represent only options to achieve the status of a skilled worker/journeyman or semi-professional.

The decisions of companies are based largely on information provided by this certification system with a sufficient degree of standardisation and transparency. But as important qualifications may exist which cannot be assessed directly, other criteria and procedures are also used. For example, a company manager in a handicraft firm may assess the occupational competence of an applicant according to his/her responses to simple questions, such as "Where were you trained?" or "What have you done since then?". In short, one should not exaggerate the significance of certificates.

Benefits of the certification system

The assessment system influences the environment, especially the labour market. If the achieved impact is an intended one, then it may be interpreted as an advantage of the assessment system.

The system of assessment in vocational training, in particular through a national final examination, offers important benefits:

– There is a standardised level of vocational qualifications and training results.

– Employers receive valid information for hiring employees.

– Standardised qualification provides the basis for negotiating wages.

– Trainees are strongly motivated for vocational training because of the advantages of the certificates.

– There is support for the implementation of new training regulations.

It may be seen from the different purposes of assessment that the emphasis here is more on maintaining standards and on selection rather than on supporting learning processes. This list of advantages, which is more hypothetical than empirically proven, can influence:

- the training system (to support learning processes and the implementation of new training regulations);
- the employment system to help employers in hiring employees;
- both educational and training systems (linking the two systems);
- society in general (providing social prestige for a large percentage of the population).

Some problems

There are also, however, some unsolved problems. The balance between the three certificates and their different functions is a matter of discussion (*i.e.* the relation between external assessment through standarised examinations, and internal assessment through learner appraisal). The representatives of the German *Länder* favour a more internal type of assessment.

The advantages of external examinations and the corresponding examination certificate (the most important one) also have their price. This kind of assessment based on the principle of standardised minimal requirements can have negative effects. For example:

- neglect of prior learning and of educational aspects;
- difficulty measuring important higher level competences;
- advanced competences as objectives of training in leading firms not being included in this uniform minimum-level standard;
- the high cost of financing the assessment system, especially external examinations.

Another problem is the "asymmetric" relationship between certification acquired in vocational and in general education.

Grades and evaluations in vocational education lead to the acquisition of certificates corresponding to concrete occupational skills. When comparing the relationships between the various skills acquired in vocational education with those in the general school system, it becomes evident that those certificates acquired in general education also have a value for the vocational education sector. For example, graduation from a lower-level secondary school may informally facilitate admittance to vocational training programmes for many occupations; in addition, this certificate – just like the school-leaving examination certificate – shortens the training period. Another example concerns the scholastic prerequisites for a career in the civil service, closely linked to the general education level. In comparison, vocational certificates are rarely taken into consideration in general education, as Pampus (1981) demonstrated in an analysis of legal regulations. He pointed out that the opportunities to acquire general education degrees qualifying for university entrance on the basis of vocational qualification are quite limited.

It is especially disturbing in the German certification system that universally acknowledged vocational qualifications such as the master craftsman certificate are not generally recognised for admission to technical college, in contrast to general education certificates. The disadvantages of the grading and evaluation systems in vocational education show that official education policy stating equality of status between vocational and general education has yet to become a reality. Efforts are being made to alter this asymmetric relationship: students with vocational certificates should also be admitted to higher education.

Debate over modifying the assessment and certification system stems from different expectations, depending on whether the system is reviewed:

– as a part of the vocational training system and of higher education (educationally oriented view);
– as an element of a company's staff management policy;
– as a tool to enhance the labour market and the relation between training and the labour market in the economy in general.

BIBLIOGRAPHY

BENNER, H. (1977), *Der Ausbildungsberuf als berufspädagogisches und bildungsökonomisches Problem*, Schrödel, Hannover.

Berufsbildungsgesetz (Vocational Training Act of the Federal Republic of Germany) (1969), 14 August 1969 (BBiG), *BGBl*, I.

Bundesausschu für Berufsbildung (1971), "Richtlinien für eine Prüfungsordnung Gemä § 41 BBiG/§ 38 HwO. Beschlu vom 9.6.1971", *Bundesarbeitsblatt*, Vol. 10.

Hauptausschu des Bundesinstituts für Berufsbildung (APLFG) (1980), "Empfehlung für die Vereinheitlichung von Prüfungsanforderungen in Ausbildungsordnungen. Beschlu vom 11.2.1980. Berlin 1980", *Berufsbildung in Wissenschaft und Praxis*, Vol. 2.

Hauptausschu des Bundesinstituts für Berufsbildung (1991), "Qualifizierung des Prüfungspersonals. Empfehlung vom 29.11.1990", *Berufsbildung in Wissenschaft und Praxis*, Vol. 20.

KELL, A. (1982), "Das Berechtigungswesen zwischen Bildungs- und Beschäftigungssystem", in Lenzen, D. (ed.), *Enzyklopädie Erziehungs-wissenschaften*, Vol. 9, Sekundarstufe II, Klett, Stuttgart, pp. 289-320.

KREEFT, H.P.J. (1991), "Examinations in Europe: Three major streams", in Luijten, A.J.M. (ed.), *Issues in Public Examinations*, Utrecht.

MACINTOSH, H.G. (1990), "External examinations", in Walberg, H.J. and Haertel, G.D. (eds.), *The International Encyclopedia of Educational Evaluation*, Pergamon Press, Oxford.

PAMPUS, K. (1981), *Die Verbindung beruflicher Qualifikationen mit allgemeinen Schulabschlüssen*, Eine Übersicht über bestehende rechtliche Regelungen, Bundesinstitut für Berufsbildung (Federal Institute for Vocational Training), Berlin.

REISSE, W. (1977), "Prüfungen und lerndiagnostische Manahmen in der beruflichen Bildung – ein systemtechnischer Ansatz zu ihrer Verbesserung", *Berufsbildung in Wissenschaft und Praxis*, 6 (4), pp. 5-10.

REISSE, W. (1989), "Mehr Zukunftsvision als Gegenwart: Die neue Prüfungspraxis für industrielle Berufe in der Metalltechnik", in *Neue Berufe – Neue Qualifikationen*, Neue industrielle Berufe in der Metalltechnik, Bundesinstitut für Berufsbildung, Nürnberg.

REISSE, W. (1991), "Abschlu- und Gesellenprüfungen als Teil des Drei-Zertifikate-Systems in der dualen Berufsausbildung", *Berufsbildung*, 45 (9/10).

REISSE, W. (1992), "Betriebliche Beurteilungen von Auszubildenden im Spannungsfeld von Lernerfolgskontrollen, Prüfungen und Zeugnissen", in Selbach, R. and Pullig, K.-K. (eds.), *Handbuch Mitarbeiterbeurteilung*, Gabler, Wiesbaden.

SCHMIDT, H. and REISSE, W. (1983), "Zensuren und Beurteilungen in der beruflichen Bildung", in Beckere, H. and Hentig, H.V. (eds.), *Zensuren, Lüge – Notwendigkeit – Alternativen* (Klett-Cotta im Ullstein-Taschenbuch), Klett, Stuttgart.

NETHERLANDS

TRAINING AND THE ASSESSMENT OF ADULTS' SKILLS AND COMPETENCES[1]

by
A.T.H. Janssen
Ministry of Education, Culture and Science, Zoetermeer

1. THE NEED FOR ASSESSMENT

A lot of knowledge and competences are not certified and therefore remain unidentified on the adult education market and on the labour market generally. Unless these qualifications are identified, it is difficult to match supply and demand in both markets. For the adult education market to be more effective and efficient, learning pathways should be linked more frequently than is the case at present. The first step would be to establish students' initial level of education. Often this cannot be determined from certificates or diplomas. Even where it is possible to do so, the qualifications reflected by the diploma are often outdated (for example in the case of women re-entering the work force). Therefore, it is important to ascertain knowledge and competences at the beginning of a learning pathway. Testing the starting level of the student makes specific ("tailored") training possible. This in turn allows training instruments to be used more effectively, avoids unnecessary use of public and private resources, and prevents students from having to focus on subject matter they have already mastered.

Thus, assessment of qualifications already acquired plays an important role in planning an individualised learning pathway; it also offers the possibility to award a certificate or diploma to persons possessing the requisite knowledge and competences according to the standards of the qualifications system. Assessment and recognition of prior learning may also prove efficient and effective in the labour market. Through recognition of knowledge and competences, the labour market becomes more transparent. Unidentified qualifications become identified. Recognition increases portability of qualifications in the labour market. Matching of supply and demand of labour is facilitated. Employers may also benefit from assessment for the training of their employees. Assessment makes tailor-made training possible and reduces the costs of training effort by the company.

2. CURRENT ASSESSMENT INSTRUMENTS IN THE NETHERLANDS

The assessment of prior learning already takes place in four different ways:

a) **National examinations for external candidates:** national examinations permit the acquisition of initial education diplomas, or certificates which constitute part of these diplomas, without having taken the corresponding courses. Thus, general secondary education diplomas and certain higher vocational education diplomas are within the reach of those who do not have the requisite school training but who do possess the required knowledge. It is also possible to take an exam as an external candidate at public institutes of general and vocational secondary education.

b) **Examinations by private educational institutions:** some private educational institutions offer, in addition to the possibility of training for a national exam, an external candidate exam or their own exam, as well as the opportunity to have prior learning assessed and in some cases recognised through the awarding of certificates.

c) **Assessment in the framework of employment services:** several job measures implemented by employment services contain an assessment component to determine the additional training needed to find a job. There are also assessment procedures for disabled persons to determine their capacities and further training requirements.

d) **Assessment in the framework of career guidance:** study and career guidance services carry out capacity tests in order to guide their clients. Placement offices use assessment techniques to find a new or more suitable job for employees who want to make a career change.

3. THE NEED FOR A NEW ASSESSMENT INSTRUMENT

Most assessment methods are aimed at specific target groups and cannot be used by every individual who wants his qualifications to be assessed. For national examinations, unless teaching is modularised, one must take the entire exam. Furthermore, it is felt that assessment should determine the individual's current qualifications, and not the educational level (diploma) to be reached. In other words, assessment should be independent of learning pathways, *i.e.* independent of when, where and how qualifications are acquired.

As long as the regular assessment system is education- instead of competency-based, it is desirable to devise an instrument that is open to any individual who wants his qualifications assessed in order to determine his additional training needs, or to award certificates or diplomas in the new system of qualifications.

A new instrument of assessment might also be very useful in implementing the government's policy to raise the educational level of the least skilled workers at least to apprenticeship level. The government views this as the necessary level for participating fully in modern society. It is called the *startkwalificatie* (starting qualification) level. Many adults (with or without jobs) who have left initial education do not yet have a *startkwalificatie*. Government and the social partners together have agreed that these adults should be given the possibility to achieve the *startkwalificatie* level. Assessment of the qualifications they already have must naturally be part of the training process.

4.   ASSESSMENT OF PRIOR LEARNING: DEVELOPMENT AND ORGANISATION

In 1993, the Minister of Education, Culture and Science set up an advisory committee to see whether a scheme for the assessment and accreditation of prior learning was desirable and possible. The committee reported to the Minister in March 1994, concluding that such a scheme would indeed be both possible and desirable. The committee believed that employers, trade unions, educational establishments, manpower services and the government could all benefit from such a scheme, which would enhance the transparency of the labour and training market, thus ensuring a better match between supply and demand, and leading to the development of more efficient learning pathways. Above all, however, such a scheme would benefit individuals who had no regular diplomas or certificates but who did have skills and experience of use to employers, which are not yet officially recognised and hence had no formal status.

In his official response to the report, the Minister agreed with the overall conclusion that recognition of skills and competences is desirable and that the scheme should serve two principal purposes:

– recognition of actual qualifications which have not yet been formalised;

– assessment of non-formal qualifications, to establish the current situation in order to achieve more efficient learning pathways to vocational qualifications.

The Minister agreed to implement assessment of prior learning (APL) experimentally in two to four pilot projects, which would on the one hand develop assessment instruments in different industrial sectors, and on the other hand investigate how APL can best be embedded in the regional educational infrastructure.

Important basic assumptions for the execution of the pilot projects are:

– APL must take place according to the standards of the newly developed National Qualifications Structure (NQS).[2]

– For the sake of portability in the labour market and transfer within the educational system, APL must lead to NQS certificates and diplomas.

– To avoid unnecessary problems for candidates without school experience, APL must be competency-based.

– APL must be person-oriented.

To meet the demands expressed by these basic assumptions, various problems have to be overcome, such as:

– As far as *transferability* of APL is concerned, we face the following dilemma. According to the NQS standards, NQS qualifications must provide a triple qualification, *i.e. i)* a professional qualification, *ii)* a transfer qualification and *iii)* a societal and cultural qualification. APL diplomas and certificates should be the same as NQS diplomas and certificates. This is to ensure portability in the labour market. This means that there will be no separate APL diplomas and certificates but only those of the NQS. Thus, if NQS diplomas and certificates acquired through initial education are transferable and portable, then NQS diplomas recognised through APL are also.

It is, however, questioned whether persons who lack school experience will be able to follow a school-based qualification track after APL. They could lack learning abilities, which would guarantee failure in a school-based qualifiying track. There-fore, it is proposed (by employers) only to provide a professional qualification, but not a transfer qualification to or within the educational system. In the Minister's view, however, APL should also serve as an instrument for further qualification within initial education. In the assessment procedure, learning abilities should also be tested. Otherwise a diploma or certificate cannot be granted. The reason for this strict approach is that separate APL qualifications will be less portable in the labour market and will have a negative influence on transparency.

– Another problem related to the introduction of APL is that the assessment system of NQS is still education-based. APL through school-based assess-ment may cause too much trouble to individuals with little school experi-ence. Therefore, *competency-based* tests must be developed according to NQS standards. These tests may serve as input for a fundamental change of the assessment system from school-based to competency-based. If the NQS assessment system is restructured, separate assessment of prior learning will not be needed any longer.

These two problems, amongst others, will be tackled in the sectoral and regional pilot projects mentioned above. Full implementation of APL will depend on the evaluation of the pilot projects in 1998.

5. CONCLUSION

APL has relevance both for individuals and institutions. The modularised NQS and APL make "tailor-made" qualification possible. Educational programmes may become shorter, which will help individuals as well as government and companies, because it will not be necessary to perform parts of a programme for which they are already qualified. Education and training may prove to be more cost-effective.

In addition, APL gives workers a more equal position in the labour market. However, when the overall educational level of the working population rises while the functional structure remains the same, it is to be expected that diploma inflation will occur.

APL may also have relevance for firms because they know better what kind of qualifications are available within their company and in the labour market. Since NQS improves the transparency of educational supply, it will become easier for firms to link their training needs to the supply.

It is expected that NQS, together with a provision for APL, will contribute a great deal to the solution of the problems of transparency, transferability, portability and relevance of diplomas. However, the real solution lies in the acceptance of NQS and APL by the actors concerned.

NOTES

1. This text has been updated since the Seminar in October 1992.

2. NQS is a single system of modularised training courses with common attainment targets, examinations, diplomas, and their associated rights. The qualification structure will create uniformity in the translation of vocational training profiles into attainment targets. This system is intended to increase transparency and recognition of qualifications.

NEW ZEALAND

THE DEVELOPMENT OF A SYSTEM
OF QUALIFICATIONS AND CERTIFICATION
BASED ON SKILLS

by

David Hood
New Zealand Qualifications Authority, Wellington

INTRODUCTION

The systems used in New Zealand to recognise knowledge and skills are undergoing substantial changes. These changes are partly driven by the radical transformations in the country's work force, and are occurring because New Zealand can no longer rely upon unprocessed natural resources to maintain its current standard of living.

Historical situation

During the 1950s, New Zealand enjoyed a relatively high standard of living compared with other OECD countries. This standard of living relied almost entirely on the production of primary products such as meat, wool, fish and timber. These products were generally exported in their natural state or with a minimum of processing.

Until the late 1970s, the knowledge and skills needed by the work force to maintain this type of production was minimal. The general education gained during three years of secondary school was adequate for most employment needs. Usually, children were able to leave secondary school at 15 and find employment.

Further training was generally only required in narrowly specialised occupations. Parents encouraged children to focus on trade training rather than higher-level technical or academic training. An apprenticeship, leading to a trade qualification, was seen as a meal ticket that would last for a lifetime. Taylorist work principles were reinforced by the unions, whose ideology narrowly limited the scope of action of each occupation.

The employment and education context from the 1950s to 1970s was shaped by an economy that relied, first, on an abundance of natural produce, second, on international markets for unprocessed primary products, and finally, on a level of processing that could employ an unskilled work force using a narrow range of skills to fulfil a limited range of duties. This industrial environment in turn contributed to a particular view of education and training, and helped shape the secondary school and post-secondary education and training systems in New Zealand.

New Zealanders have always valued education and training. However, the type and level of education and training desirable has often been questioned. As long as it was possible to obtain employment with low or no qualifications, secondary school participation rates remained low. As recently as 1981, only 53 per cent of those entering school attended the fourth year of secondary school and only 16 per cent attended the fifth year. The low participation rates can also be attributed to a selective national examination system which aimed to limit participation. The School Certificate examination taken in the third year of secondary school was designed to select the best individuals. Through statistical manipulations this exam opened doors to further education for some but closed them for others. High built-in failure rates ensured that only the "cream" went on to higher education.

This situation also helped define the curriculum. The subjects taught in upper secondary school were designed to cater for the academic careers of the minority. For the majority, excluded from this path, there was little motivation to stay in school.

The current situation

It is no longer possible to maintain a high standard of living with a poorly qualified work force. New Zealand's standard of living has been declining. Most workers have a low level of qualifications, and unemployment is high. A recent study has shown that 72 per cent of those unemployed for more than two years have no qualifications. The industrial future for New Zealand lies in actively competing in a world market, particularly in the manufacturing, finance and information sectors.

New Zealand will continue to rely heavily on natural resources. However, raising the standard of living implies increasing the value of these resources. New skills must be emphasized to meet the needs of the growing service sector. These skills must focus on quality, cost control, marketing, language, and the application of technology. New Zealand's successful manufacturers have focused on high-value, high-technology products, particularly those that can be produced in small production runs. These changes within industry have entailed dramatic consequences for the work force in the last ten years.

First, the old Taylorist methods that have determined the industrial relations systems are being increasingly swept away. Flexibility is crucial to successfully meeting customer needs. This increasing departure from a Taylorist work force has been reinforced by a move away from a national industrial pay system based on occupations, to company-based agreements, which also tend to index salaries to workers' knowledge and skill levels. Company agreements identify fewer categories of workers and encourage employees to further develop and upgrade their skills. Workers in these firms generally have a wider range of duties and more responsibility.

Second, there has been a dramatic decline in the demand for unskilled workers and manual jobs. There is a realisation that the minimum level of general education gained during the compulsory years of schooling is not enough. Instead, lifelong learning and the development of a "learning culture", are being encouraged. This has resulted in a marked increase in secondary school participation rates. In addition, workers are expressing the desire to undertake further training to adapt to changes in the work place. Finally, in today's global market, only the most competitive can survive. Consequently, industry has begun to focus more on quality. This has led to the identification of work force standards of performance, and the development of training systems to ensure those performance levels are achieved.

1.   REFORM OF THE EDUCATION SECTOR

The trends in industry have led to reform of the systems for recognising knowledge and skills in New Zealand. These changes in the work force did not occur overnight. Neither was the government's response to them immediate. In the education sector a number of reports have appeared over the past decade in response to these changes. The pace of change in the education sector, however, has increased over the last few years. Between 1986 and 1989 the government undertook a review of all previous policy initiatives which led to a major restructuring of the post-compulsory education and training system. Several new education agencies were created, each with a specific function:

- The Ministry of Education provides policy advice to the Minister of Education.
- The New Zealand Qualifications Authority co-ordinates the development of an accessible and flexible qualifications system.
- The Education and Training Support Agency co-ordinates the development of vocational training systems.
- A number of other agencies focus on information needs, special education services and the quality of school-based training.

The new national Qualifications Authority

In a country of little more than three million people, more than 50 different bodies were involved in the qualifications field. These bodies often used markedly different systems to assess and recognise knowledge and skills, even in similar areas. Three different systems operated at the upper secondary school level alone.

The students who succeeded in passing the highly selective school examination system found that gaining higher levels of education and skills was often limited by the qualification systems.

Knowledge and skills acquired and assessed under a trade-level qualification often had to be repeated and reassessed at the technician level and again when moving from the technician to the degree level. At worst, knowledge and skills were not given recognition elsewhere in the same sector.

Perhaps the greatest disadvantage of the previous vocational qualification system was that it was not always controlled by industry. Industry input was relatively strong in the crafts trades but in most other sectors the system was primarily established and operated either by government agencies or by training institutions. In many cases the qualifications were out of date or focused on the perceived rather than actual needs of industry. The system therefore did not effectively meet the requirements of the users of national qualifications. The need was widely felt for a single qualifications authority which would be responsible for all nationally recognised qualifications, from senior secondary school to university.

With the establishment of the New Zealand Qualifications Authority, the country now has such a body. Its main functions are:

- to develop a framework for the co-ordination of all qualifications in post-compulsory education and training so that they have a purpose and relationship to one another which the public and students can understand;

- to oversee the setting and regular review of standards as they relate to qualifications;

- to ensure that qualifications acquired in New Zealand are recognised abroad and that overseas qualifications are recognised in this country;

- to administer national examinations, both at secondary school and university levels.

The new qualifications system

Since its creation in July 1990, the Qualifications Authority has not only had to continue operating the systems that it inherited but also to address the problems caused by the great diversity of qualification systems. To this end, the Authority spent two years developing a National Qualifications Framework.

This framework was developed after consultation, both nationally and internationally. It builds on what the Authority believes is international best practice, and has benefited in particular from the assistance of SCOTVEC, NCVQ and the Australian National Training Board. The system in New Zealand may be unique, however, in being the first to cover both vocational and general education. The National Qualifications Framework has four main pillars:

- It is made up of "unit standards" according to a modular system. Each unit standard contains a number of learning objectives and performance criteria that together comprise precise national standards.

- It is a system that uses assessment methods to measure performance against the standards contained within each unit.

- It enables assessment to occur outside of formal training systems. It should allow and encourage the recognition of prior learning.

- It has a common system of quality control relating to all assessment contexts. It applies to all post-compulsory education and training – that is, it incorporates assessment which occurs in schools, polytechnical institutes, private training establishments, colleges of education (for teacher training) and the work place. A common quality control system is important in guaranteeing that assessment is uniform across these diverse sectors.

The building blocks of the framework – unit standards – are assigned to one of eight levels. Level 1 is open-ended to encompass all initial learning (see Appendix 1).

Qualifications consist of tailored packages of units which are normally determined by professional and industry groups. It is also possible for individual education and training providers, or business enterprises, to create their own. For example, the Toyota motor company could promote its own package of units making up the Toyota Certificate of Engineering. In this way, if the knowledge and skills standards needed by Toyota vary from the standards contained within the units making up the National Certificate of Engineering, they can be catered for within the system.

There is a logical sequence of qualification names. Under the eight-level system, qualifications falling within the first four levels are called National Certificates. Qualifications falling within levels five to seven are called National Diplomas. Initial university degrees are placed at level seven. There are thus only three nationally recognised qualification titles – National Certificate, National Diploma and Degree.

The National Qualifications Framework does not contain one single secondary school qualification. The National Certificates available to teenagers in schools provide tertiary qualifications. A few of these certificates can be completed at school but many require further education or training either through higher institutions or in the work place. This will send a clear signal to young people that school-based learning is a pathway to further learning and lifelong qualifications.

It is noteworthy that the Qualifications Authority does not see itself as a centralised and bureaucratic agency running a system for the whole country. Rather, a Qualifications Framework has been put in place that the community, industry and education and training providers alike, understand and wish to work within. Participation, and in particular the involvement of industry and professional groups, is an important aspect of the National Qualifications Framework.

The national standards contained within each unit have to be endorsed by the national groups concerned. No standards are set for industry without their endorsement. All standards are set for a maximum of five years. After this period they are to be referred back to the appropriate national bodies for re-endorsement or replacement. In this manner, the qualification system meets the current and future needs of society.

2.   OTHER DEVELOPMENTS

Several parallel developments will affect the success of the implementation of the National Qualifications Framework. One of these is the recent reform of industry training sponsored by the public authorities. Through the Industry Training Act, passed in July 1992, the government implemented mechanisms that will lead to the recognition of industry training organisations for each industry. They will be responsible for developing unit standards, systems to monitor training, and systems to assess trainees.

The government has tended, through the Industry Training Act, to provide subsidies only for training that leads to qualifications recognised in the National Qualifications Framework. A Training Opportunities Programme provides training to long-term unemployed and young people with low qualification levels. This programme also ties all education and training to the National Qualifications Framework.

3.   IMPLEMENTATION OF THE FRAMEWORK

Industry initiatives

The principal sectors of industry have begun to develop national qualifications for inclusion in the National Qualifications Framework. Initial developments have focused on the first four levels of the framework, with some developments at the higher levels.

General education

The main subjects of general education taken by students in upper secondary school were integrated into the new system over a two-year period. During this time, teachers were trained in new assessment methods and systems of quality control.

A number of research projects have been initiated to develop systems enabling the assessment of prior learning. In addition, a national quality control system applying to institutions that deliver national qualifications has been devised. This will be implemented progressively in tandem with the National Qualifications Framework, and a system will also be developed to ensure the quality of work place assessment (see Appendix 2).

4. SUMMARY

The new qualifications framework is made up of "unit standards" according to a modular system. Each unit standard contains a number of learning outcomes and performance criteria that together comprise specific national standards. The framework uses assessment methods which measure performance against the standards contained within each unit. It enables assessment to be made outside of formal training systems. It will allow, and encourages, the recognition of prior learning. It has a common system of quality control that applies to all assessment situations. The new qualifications framework applies to all post-compulsory education and training.

Appendix 1

DEFINITION OF PERFORMANCE LEVELS

The following definitions of levels are designed to establish profiles for matching unit standards to the qualifications framework on a "best-fit" basis. The level at which there is the greatest correspondence between the outcomes of the unit and the criteria listed below is the level at which the unit should be presented for assessment in view of registration in the national framework database. It must be emphasized that the criteria are not universally applicable and are provided for guidance only. The appropriate level will ultimately be determined by negotiation between the relevant national standards group and the Qualifications Authority.

Potential users of the definitions should take into account that the levels descriptions will be modified in the light of practice and further research; such changes will, however, have little impact on units and qualifications already registered. The New Zealand Qualifications Authority is undertaking research nationally and with Australia, with the aim of creating a qualifications structure common to the two countries. International developments and accords are also likely to affect these definitions.

GENERAL DEFINITIONS

Level 1: Units completed at this level constitute a foundation for further education and training, including on-the-job training, which in turn leads to recognised qualifications.

Level 2: Units completed at this level lead to further education and training at higher levels and to certificated qualifications for crafts or trades.

Level 3: Units completed at this level lead to further education and training at higher levels and to certificated qualifications for skilled occupations, crafts and trades.

Level 4: Units completed at this level lead to further education and training at higher levels and to certificated qualifications for advanced craft or technical occupations.

Level 5: Units completed at this level lead to further education and training at higher levels and to certificated qualifications for advanced craft or technical occupations.

Level 6: Units completed at this level lead to further education and training at higher levels and to certificated qualifications for senior technical, paraprofessional and technological occupations.

Level 7: Units completed at this level lead to further education and training at higher levels and to certificated qualifications equivalent to the first degree (bachelor's degree) for academic, professional and managerial occupations.

Level 8: Units completed at this level lead to further education and training at higher levels and to certificated qualifications (master's degree, Doctor of Philosophy) for higher academic, professional and managerial occupations.

Appendix 2

QUALITY CONTROL SYSTEMS FOR THE NATIONAL QUALIFICATIONS FRAMEWORK

The quality control system for nationally recognised qualifications is based on five elements:

- registration of private training institutions and recognition of public training establishments;

- registration of units and qualifications;

- accreditation of training providers;

- ongoing control of assessment;

- audit.

REGISTRATION OF PRIVATE TRAINING PROVIDERS AND RECOGNITION OF GOVERNMENT TRAINING ESTABLISHMENTS

Under the Education Amendment Act 1990, a private training institution must be registered in order to be eligible for government funding. These establishments must also be registered if they wish to offer courses of three months or longer to foreign students.

Registration is the first step for the private sector, in the Qualifications Authority's National Qualifications Framework quality control system. Registration confirms that a private training institution is effective in two key areas of quality control: organisation and teaching. The first ensures the stability of the establishment and the fairness of its relationship with students. The second ensures that staff understand the standards of educational quality required and that the institution has policies and procedures to implement these effectively. Recognition of public training institutions involves a similar evaluation process, albeit less rigorous in recognition of the long history of these institutions in providing high-quality training.

Registration is undertaken by an officer of the Qualifications Authority and involves an evaluation of documentation supplied by the applicant. The process can also include a visit by the officer to the premises of the applicant institution.

REGISTRATION OF UNITS AND QUALIFICATIONS

Registration of units and qualifications is the process of formally accepting units and qualifications in the National Qualifications Framework. It requires an evaluation of the technical quality of each unit and confirmation that the standards set out in individual units and qualifications are endorsed by the national user group.

During the process of registration of units and qualifications, options for accreditation and control are discussed and the role of national industry groups is determined. Once units and qualifications are registered, they are available to schools and to registered public and private training institutions seeking accreditation. An officer of the Qualifications Authority evaluates the unit(s)'s technical quality, ensures they are endorsed by the user group, negotiates aspects of the quality control system applying to the unit(s) and enters the accepted units into a national database.

ACCREDITATION OF TRAINING PROVIDERS

Institutions and private training establishments are required, under the Education Amendment Act 1990, to be accredited *a)* before they can deliver nationally recognised courses, and *b)* if they provide courses for foreign students which last three months or longer. Accreditation requires a judgement regarding the ability of an institution or private training establishment to deliver and assess the learning objectives contained in a nationally recognised qualification.

The depth of the accreditation process will vary according to the levels in the framework. The accreditation process for Level 1 units is not as rigorous as that applied to units at a higher level. The new accreditation process, approved by the board of the Qualifications Authority on 27 July 1992, therefore has a number of options. These are:

- *the use of "standard setters"* to provide technical expertise, in the accreditation of education and training providers (*i.e.* for members of Industry Training Organisations);

- the *type of accreditation* process decided on by those standard setters; this might range from an evaluation of a written submission to a visit by an evaluation panel;

- the *level of accreditation* sought; this will range from accreditation for one unit to accreditation for all units in the framework, including future units (general accreditation).

ONGOING CONTROL OF ASSESSMENT

This refers to the mechanisms that guarantee the fairness, validity and consistency of assessment. Once the control system is agreed to by the Qualifications Authority, it is administered by the standard setters working in partnership with the training providers. Where necessary, the Authority offers to run a control system under contract to the standard-setting body. When this is the case, it is competing in a market situation.

AUDIT

A quality audit is a process for ensuring the effective performance of an institution's or private training establishment's overall quality control system. The Qualifications Authority sees the audit role as its main function in the quality control system.

HOLISTIC NATURE OF THE QUALITY CONTROL SYSTEM

It should be noted that each element of the quality control system contributes to the whole. For example, the process of registering units and qualifications ensures that units are well written and the standards they contain measurable. Easily understood and measurable standards in turn help training providers to ensure the quality of their training services and assessment. Well-written unit standards also contribute to the consistency of assessment (control).

As the system works as a whole, it is possible to vary parts of the system while ensuring the overall quality of training services and assessment. For any given unit standard it is possible to have *either* a light accreditation and a rigorous control process *or* a rigorous accreditation with a light control process, and still maintain the levels of quality under both options.

UNITED STATES

IN SEARCH OF A NATIONAL SYSTEM OF QUALIFICATIONS

by

Winifred I. Warnat
Division of Vocational-Technical Education
Department of Education, Washington

The purpose of this paper is to provide a synthetic analysis of developments in the United States that are laying the groundwork for a national voluntary system of standards, assessment and certification of occupational skills and competences. Decentralisation and diversity, all elements of the United States' national character, are key features of the training system which is described in detail in *Vocational Education and Training for Youth: Towards Coherent Policy and Practice* (OECD, 1994).

1. THE SKILL STANDARDS MOVEMENT

Vocational-technical education in the United States has just begun to seriously address the assessment, certification and recognition of occupational skills and competences within the framework of standards – programme standards, performance standards, industry-based skill standards.

The Job Training Partnership Act

The precursor to the skill standards movement was the Job Training Partnership Act legislated in 1982. JTPA is the largest federally supported out-of-school job training programme in the United States. It has as its target unemployed and hard-to-employ adults and youth who are welfare recipients. Administered by the Department of Labor, JTPA is the first federal law to specify programme performance measures and standards to determine results of programme participation for both adults and young people. Two performance measures are specified: *i)* the increase in employment and earnings; and *ii)* reductions in welfare dependence. The performance standards designated in JTPA include placement and retention in unsubsidised employment; increased earnings; and reduction in the number of individuals and families receiving welfare payments. Additional standards for youth programmes include attainment of recognised employment competences; elementary, secondary and post-secondary school completion or equivalent; and enrolment in other training programmes, apprenticeship or military service.

The Perkins Act

With the enactment of the Carl D. Perkins Vocational and Applied Technology Education Act of 1990 (Perkins Act), the standards movement in VOTEC officially started. The Perkins Act, administered by the Department of Education, is the primary federally legislated authority for vocational-technical education in the United States. All states receive federal funds from the Perkins Act. Considerable groundwork had been done in the 1970s, when VOTEC became a prime mover in the competence-based education movement. A number of initiatives were undertaken to develop and implement competence-based vocational curricula. The effort began enthusiastically but had waned considerably by the mid-1980s. Then, in the late 1980s, the re-authorisation process for the Perkins Act placed heavy emphasis on accountability and quality in VOTEC, with the push for skill standards.

The state system of standards and measures

Under the Perkins Act, every state receiving federal funds is required to develop and implement an accountability system of core performance standards and measures. The Perkins Act requires that each state system include:

- measures of learning and competence gains, including student progress in the achievement of basic and more advanced academic skills;
- at least one of the following performance measures:
  - competence attainment;
  - job or work skill attainment;
  - retention in school or completion of secondary school or its equivalent;
  - placement into additional training or education, military service or employment.

Although different standards and measures may be established for secondary and post-secondary programmes, the system is to be applied at both levels. It will also include incentives or adjustments to encourage service to special populations, as well as procedures for using existing resources and methods developed in other programmes receiving federal funds, namely JTPA. The standards developed by each state are to be used by the localities to evaluate their Perkins-supported VOTEC programmes on an annual basis. To date, over 40 of the states have begun implementation of their accountability systems.

Development of business and education standards

The Perkins Act also provides the authority to pursue and develop proposed national standards for occupational competences in select industries and trades. The standards to be established include:

- the major divisions or speciality areas identified within the occupation studies;
- the minimum hours of study to become competent in those divisions or specialities;
- the minimum tools and equipment required;
- the minimum qualifications for instructional staff;
- the minimum tasks to be included in any course of study claiming to prepare individuals for those select areas (US Congress, 1990).

America's choice

In 1990, further impetus to the skill standards movement was provided by a provocative report, *America's Choice: High Skills or Low Wages!* (Commission on the Skills of the American Work force, 1990). The report presents a new paradigm involving education, employers and the community in preparing and maintaining a quality work force. Central to the paradigm is a system of assessment, certification and recognition of occupational skills and competences. Credentials proposed include an initial certificate of mastery, technical and professional certificates, associate degrees and industry-based skill certificates. Also proposed as part of the system are performance-based assessment standards, a cumulative assessment system and a certification system. The report sets the stage for SCANS.

SCANS

The Secretary's Commission on Achieving Necessary Skills (SCANS) was established by the Secretary of Labor in February 1990, to examine the demands of the work place and determine whether the current and future work force is capable of meeting those demands. The charge of SCANS was to address the kinds and level of skills required to enter employment. In that regard, it was asked to: *i)* define the skills needed for employment; *ii)* propose acceptable levels in those skills; *iii)* suggest effective ways to assess proficiency; and *iv)* develop a strategy to disseminate the findings to education, employers and families (SCANS, 1992).

SCANS is having a significant impact on the skill standards movement. More than any initiative to date, SCANS has focused on what it refers to as "work place know-how" that it defines as having two elements – competences and a foundation.

The five competences and three-part foundation are provided in Appendices 1 and 2.

After defining work place competences and know-how skills, SCANS concluded its mission by recommending a plan of action of which a key component is a system of standards setting and assessment. Elements of the assessment system include a certificate of initial mastery, a cumulative résumé of skill attainment, and employment-based assessments (Silvestri and Lukasiewicz, 1991, pp. 64-94).

Voluntary industry-based skill standards and certification

With the work of SCANS completed, the Department of Labor, with the Department of Education, began a new initiative addressing voluntary industry-based skill standards and certification.

In the spring of 1992, the two departments held a series of five public hearings across the country to obtain reactions to the development of voluntary, industry-based skill standards and certification from the key stakeholder groups: government, education, industry, organised labour, joint labour-management committees, community-based organisations, private citizens and service providers.

Nearly 70 existing school- and work-based approaches to skill standards, assessment and certification were identified by the hearing respondents. Among the most frequently noted school-based models were the following.

Vocational-Technical Education Consortium of States (V-TECS)

V-TECS is a consortium of 22 states begun in 1973. The organisation is funded by its member states. V-TECS has developed 160 catalogues listing skills and performance objectives matched to the *Dictionary of Occupational Titles* (DOT) codes. The catalogues are used by states as a basis for developing curriculum materials primarily for secondary vocational education programmes. Member states that agree to draw up a catalogue must use the V-TECS development model, which requires skill verification by employers (Employment and Training Administration, 1992).

National Institute for Automotive Service Excellence (ASE)

ASE provides competence-level tests in all the areas of competence required for automotive repair, auto-body repair, and medium/heavy truck repair. These tests are administered nationwide twice a year and provide employed technicians with a means of proving journeyman-level competence. ASE certifies entry-level training programmes on the basis of industry-developed standards. It also offers an automotive technicians' training certification programme through its National Automotive Technicians Education Foundation (NATEF) used by both secondary and post-secondary institutions. NATEF works primarily with secondary programmes. The evaluation process includes self-evaluation, on-site evaluations and re-certification after five years. For the ASE technician testing, the American College Testing Services, Iowa, is used for administration and evaluation (Employment and Training Administration, 1992).

"Tech Prep" education

Tech Prep education is an alternative to the college prep course of study. It prepares the student for a highly skilled technical occupation that allows either direct entry into the work place as a qualified technician, or continuation with further education leading to baccalaureate and advanced degrees. Tech prep is a four-year sequence of study beginning in the 11th year of high school through two years of post-secondary occupational education, culminating in a certificate or associate degree. It is a combined secondary and post-secondary programme based on a formal articulation agreement, providing students with a non-duplicative sequence of progressive achievement leading to competences in a tech prep programme. Preparation is provided in at least one field of engineering technology, applied science, mechanical, industrial or practical art or trade, agriculture, health or business. The Perkins Act provides funds to all states to develop and implement tech prep education.

Among the work-based approaches identified, apprenticeship was noted most frequently and two industry-specific approaches repeatedly.

Apprenticeship

Apprenticeship in the United States is on-the-job training combined with related instruction in occupations that require skilled and versatile workers. Apprenticeship programmes are operated by employers, employer associations, and jointly by management and labour on a voluntary basis. The formal United States apprenticeship system was established in 1937 with the passing of the National Apprenticeship Act. Currently, there are approximately 283 000 registered apprentices in more than 820 apprenticeship occupations. Of those, 7.1 per cent are women, 22.5 per cent minority, and approximately 80 per cent in the construction sector. The Federal government's role in apprenticeship is largely one of promotion and technical assistance. At present, over 43 000 programmes are registered with state or federal apprenticeship agencies.

Professional Truck Drivers Institute of America, Inc. (PTDIA)

PTDIA has identified standards and certification programmes for truck drivers. Specifically, the PTDIA programme is a voluntary, industry-based set of skill standards that are tied to measurable, performance-oriented and readily-accessible outcomes, developed independently of any training provider. The Institute developed a certification programme based upon the Federal Highway Administration's Bureau of Motor Carrier Safety's 1984 "Proposed Minimum Standards for Training Tractor-Trailer Drivers". The programme, which is voluntary, evaluates the effectiveness of content and quality of entry-level training courses. PTDIA has certified courses at 62 institutions in 25 states, representing an estimated 15-20 per cent of the total number of driver-training courses (Employment and Training Administration, 1992).

Oral and written testimony was received from 210 individuals representing the eight stakeholder groups. From the testimonies, seven dominant policy issues emerged:

- *Development of standards:* What are the major choices to be made in defining skill standards? Should they be modular? Technical? Generic? What is the appropriate structure and level of skill standards?

- *Applicability of standards:* How should skill standards be benchmarked to best practice? What are the civil rights implications? What is the relationship of skill standards to existing licensing and occupational regulations? What institutional structures may be required to maintain the currency of standards?

- *Training to industry standards:* What will facilitate the adoption of standards by educators and training providers? How are standards to be successfully integrated with the vocational education system? With existing work force preparation programmes? What process of accreditation will ensure integrity while minimising bureaucracy?

- *Competence-based assessment:* What methods are the most suitable for competence assessment? What is known about the validity, reliability, fairness and costs of these methods? Who should develop and conduct the assessments?

- *Skill certification:* Who should be the certifying body? Should the certifications be modular? Linked to existing qualifications?

- *Quality assurance:* In developing and maintaining skill standards, how can consistency and portability be maintained across industries and within occupational groups which transcend industries? How should standards and certification arrangements be maintained?

- *Incentives:* What are the public and private benefits of standards? What are the incentive options? potential disincentives? (Employment and Training Administration, 1992).

2. CONCLUSIONS AND CONSIDERATIONS FOR IMPLEMENTATION

As the plethora of actions indicate, the United States is working to establish a national voluntary system of standards, assessment and certification that recognises occupational skills and competences. It is a difficult, long-term process; the United States is just beginning. Some progress has been made. The issue is on the national agenda. The players have been identified. Exploratory activities are under way. Legislative action is precipitating systems development.

The complexities of implementing broad-based occupational-relevant standards, assessment and certification in the United States make it difficult to draw conclusions. Many factors must be taken into account. Based on the overview of ongoing efforts in this country, attention is drawn to three areas:

- *Decentralisation*: in the free enterprise system, business demands independence and minimal control. The focus of government is on states' rights and local autonomy, with minimal federal intervention and control. So, while all states are mandated to develop VOTEC programme performance-standards systems, there is minimal planned co-ordination. In a voluntary system, businesses may or may not choose to participate. Many have already developed their own industry-specific skill qualifications.

- *Diversity*: the lack of homogeneity in the United States limits uniformity in process or outcomes where standards, assessment and certification are involved. There is no single "right way". A multiplicity of approaches and models addressing them already exist and more are forthcoming. All available pathways should be equally desirable and still keep options open while continuing to address the nation's human resource needs.

- *Diffusion*: systems development is fragmented. The synergy between education and employment is strained. Separate systems are being suggested for standards, for assessment and for credentialling. Innumerable programmes and skill standards are being developed in microcosm without co-ordination or integration. The United States is in a flurry of activity to establish a national voluntary system of skill standards, assessment and credentialling, and is moving in several disconnected directions at once. Perhaps there is a need for a structure of systems, incrementally developed, which utilise co-ordination by consensus.

FIVE COMPETENCES

RESOURCES: IDENTIFIES, ORGANISES, PLANS, AND ALLOCATES RESOURCES

- *Time:* selects goal-relevant activities, ranks them, allocates time, and prepares and follows schedules.

- *Money:* uses or prepares budgets, makes forecasts, keeps records, and makes adjustments to meet objectives.

- *Material and facilities:* acquires, stores, allocates, and uses materials or space efficiently.

- *Human resources:* assesses skills and distributes work accordingly, evaluates performance and provides feedback.

INTERPERSONAL: WORKS WITH OTHERS

- *Participates as member of a team:* contributes to group effort.

- Teaches others new skills.

- *Serves clients/customers:* works to satisfy customers' expectations.

- *Exercises leadership:* communicates ideas to justify position, persuades and convinces others, responsibly challenges existing procedures and policies.

- *Negotiates:* works toward agreements involving exchange of resources, resolves divergent interests.

- *Works with diversity:* works well with men and women from diverse backgrounds.

INFORMATION: ACQUIRES AND USES INFORMATION

- Acquires and evaluates information.

- Organises and maintains information.

- Interprets and communicates information.

- Uses computers to process information.

SYSTEMS: UNDERSTANDS COMPLEX INTERRELATIONSHIPS

– *Understands systems:* knows how social, organisational and technological systems work, and operates effectively with them.

– *Monitors and corrects performance:* distinguishes trends, predicts impacts on system operations, diagnoses deviations in systems' performance, and corrects malfunctions.

– *Improves or designs systems:* suggests modifications to existing systems, and develops new or alternative systems to improve performance.

TECHNOLOGY: WORKS WITH A VARIETY OF TECHNOLOGIES

– *Selects technology:* chooses procedures, tools or equipment, including computers and related technologies.

– *Applies technology to task:* understands overall intent and proper procedures for set-up and operation of equipment.

– *Maintains and troubleshoots equipment:* prevents, identifies or solves problems with equipment, including computers and other technologies.

Appendix 2

A THREE-PART FOUNDATION

BASIC SKILLS: READS, WRITES, PERFORMS ARITHMETIC AND MATHEMATICAL OPERATIONS, LISTENS AND SPEAKS

- *Reading:* locates, understands and interprets written information in prose and in documents such as manuals, graphs and schedules.

- *Writing:* communicates thoughts, ideas, information and messages in writing; and creates documents such as letters, directions, manuals, reports, graphs, and flow charts.

- *Arithmetic/mathematics:* performs basic computations, and deals with practical problems by choosing appropriately from a variety of mathematical techniques.

- *Listening:* receives, attends to, interprets, and responds to verbal messages and other cues.

- *Speaking:* organises ideas and communicates orally.

THINKING SKILLS: THINKS CREATIVELY, MAKES DECISIONS, SOLVES PROBLEMS, VISUALISES, KNOWS HOW TO LEARN, AND REASONS

- *Creative thinking:* generates new ideas.

- *Decision making:* specifies goals and constraints, generates alternatives, considers risks, and evaluates and chooses best alternative.

- *Problem solving:* recognises problems, and devises and implements plan of action.

- *Seeing things in the mind's eye:* organises and processes symbols, pictures, graphs, objects and other information.

- *Knowing how to learn:* uses efficient learning techniques to acquire and apply new knowledge and skills.

- *Reasoning:* discovers a rule or principle underlying the relationship between two or more objects, and applies it when solving a problem.

PERSONAL QUALITIES: DISPLAYS RESPONSIBILITY, SELF-ESTEEM, SOCIABILITY, SELF-MANAGEMENT, AND INTEGRITY AND HONESTY

- *Responsibility:* exerts a high level of effort and perseveres towards goal attainment.

- *Self-esteem:* believes in own self-worth and maintains a positive view of self.

- *Sociability:* demonstrates understanding, friendliness, adaptability, empathy and politeness in group settings.

- *Self-management:* assesses self accurately, sets personal goals, monitors progress, and exhibits self-control.

- *Integrity/honesty:* chooses ethical courses of action.

BIBLIOGRAPHY

CAREY, M. L. and FROUKLEN, J. C. (1991), "Industry output and job growth continues to slow into next century", *Monthly Labor Review*, 114, 11 November.

Commission on the Skills of the American Work force (1990), *America's Choice: High Skills or Low Wages!*, National Center on Education and the Economy, Rochester, New York.

Employment and Training Administration (1992), *Analysis: Public Dialogue on Voluntary Industry-Based Skill Standards and Certification*, Draft, US Department of Labor, Washington, DC, September.

National Center for Education Statistics (1992), "Education at a glance", US Department of Education, Washington, DC, March.

National Center for Education Statistics (1992), *Vocational Education in the United States: 1969-1990*, US Department of Education, Washington, DC, April.

OECD (1994), *Vocational Education and Training for Youth: Towards Coherent Policy and Practice*, Paris.

Secretary's Commission on Achieving Necessary Skills (SCANS) (1992), *Learning a Living: A Blueprint for High Performance*, US Department of Labor, Washington, DC, April.

SILVESTRI, G. and LUKASIEWICZ, J. (1991), "Occupational employment projections", *Monthly Labor Review*, 114, 11 November.

US Congress (1982), *Job Training Partnership Act*, 97th Congress, Washington, DC, 13 October.

US Congress (1990), *Carl D. Perkins: Vocational and Applied Technology Education Act Amendments of 1990*, 101st Congress, Washington, DC, 25 September.

Also available

Apprenticeship: Which Way Forward?
(91 94 04 1) ISBN 92-64-14294-0, November 1994, 165 pp.
France: FF 160   Other countries: FF 210   US$ 38   DM 63

Vocational Education and Training for Youth:
Towards Coherent Policy and Practice
(91 94 03 1) ISBN 92-64-14285-1, November 1994, 180 pp.
France: FF 170   Other countries: FF 220   US$ 41   DM 67

Vocational Training in Germany: Modernisation and Responsiveness
(91 94 05 1) ISBN 92-64-14301-7, November 1994, 134 pp.
France: FF 120   Other countries: FF 155   US$ 29   DM 48

Vocational Training in the Netherlands: Reform and Innovation
(91 94 06 1) ISBN 92-64-14-14298-3, November 1994, 220 pp.
France: FF 195   Other countries: FF 250   US$ 48   DM 72

Prices charged at the OECD Bookshop.
The OECD CATALOGUE OF PUBLICATIONS and supplements will be sent free of charge
on request addressed either to OECD Publications,
or to the OECD Distributor in your country.

MAIN SALES OUTLETS OF OECD PUBLICATIONS
PRINCIPAUX POINTS DE VENTE DES PUBLICATIONS DE L'OCDE

ARGENTINA – ARGENTINE
Carlos Hirsch S.R.L.
Galería Güemes, Florida 165, 4° Piso
1333 Buenos Aires   Tel. (1) 331.1787 y 331.2391
Telefax: (1) 331.1787

AUSTRALIA – AUSTRALIE
D.A. Information Services
648 Whitehorse Road, P.O.B 163
Mitcham, Victoria 3132   Tel. (03) 9210.7777
Telefax: (03) 9210.7788

AUSTRIA – AUTRICHE
Gerold & Co.
Graben 31
Wien 1   Tel. (0222) 533.50.14
Telefax: (0222) 512.47.31.29

BELGIUM – BELGIQUE
Jean De Lannoy
Avenue du Roi 202 Koningslaan
B-1060 Bruxelles   Tel. (02) 538.51.69/538.08.41
Telefax: (02) 538.08.41

CANADA
Renouf Publishing Company Ltd.
1294 Algoma Road
Ottawa, ON K1B 3W8   Tel. (613) 741.4333
Telefax: (613) 741.5439
Stores:
61 Sparks Street
Ottawa, ON K1P 5R1   Tel. (613) 238.8985
12 Adelaide Street West
Toronto, ON M5H 1L6   Tel. (416) 363.3171
Telefax: (416)363.59.63

Les Éditions La Liberté Inc.
3020 Chemin Sainte-Foy
Sainte-Foy, PQ G1X 3V6   Tel. (418) 658.3763
Telefax: (418) 658.3763

Federal Publications Inc.
165 University Avenue, Suite 701
Toronto, ON M5H 3B8   Tel. (416) 860.1611
Telefax: (416) 860.1608

Les Publications Fédérales
1185 Université
Montréal, QC H3B 3A7   Tel. (514) 954.1633
Telefax: (514) 954.1635

CHINA – CHINE
China National Publications Import
Export Corporation (CNPIEC)
16 Gongti E. Road, Chaoyang District
P.O. Box 88 or 50
Beijing 100704 PR   Tel. (01) 506.6688
Telefax: (01) 506.3101

CHINESE TAIPEI – TAIPEI CHINOIS
Good Faith Worldwide Int'l. Co. Ltd.
9th Floor, No. 118, Sec. 2
Chung Hsiao E. Road
Taipei   Tel. (02) 391.7396/391.7397
Telefax: (02) 394.9176

**CZECH REPUBLIC –
RÉPUBLIQUE TCHÈQUE**
Artia Pegas Press Ltd.
Narodni Trida 25
POB 825
111 21 Praha 1   Tel. (2) 242 246 04
Telefax: (2) 242 278 72

DENMARK – DANEMARK
Munksgaard Book and Subscription Service
35, Nørre Søgade, P.O. Box 2148
DK-1016 København K   Tel. (33) 12.85.70
Telefax: (33) 12.93.87

EGYPT – ÉGYPTE
Middle East Observer
41 Sherif Street
Cairo   Tel. 392.6919
Telefax: 360-6804

FINLAND – FINLANDE
Akateeminen Kirjakauppa
Keskuskatu 1, P.O. Box 128
00100 Helsinki
Subscription Services/Agence d'abonnements :
P.O. Box 23
00371 Helsinki   Tel. (358 0) 121 4416
Telefax: (358 0) 121.4450

FRANCE
OECD/OCDE
Mail Orders/Commandes par correspondance :
2, rue André-Pascal
75775 Paris Cedex 16   Tel. (33-1) 45.24.82.00
Telefax: (33-1) 49.10.42.76
Telex: 640048 OCDE
Internet: Compte.PUBSINQ @ oecd.org
Orders via Minitel, France only/
Commandes par Minitel, France exclusivement :
36 15 OCDE
OECD Bookshop/Librairie de l'OCDE :
33, rue Octave-Feuillet
75016 Paris   Tel. (33-1) 45.24.81.81
(33-1) 45.24.81.67
Dawson
B.P. 40
91121 Palaiseau Cedex   Tel. 69.10.47.00
Telefax : 64.54.83.26

Documentation Française
29, quai Voltaire
75007 Paris   Tel. 40.15.70.00

Economica
49, rue Héricart
75015 Paris   Tel. 45.78.12.92
Telefax : 40.58.15.70

Gibert Jeune (Droit-Économie)
6, place Saint-Michel
75006 Paris   Tel. 43.25.91.19

Librairie du Commerce International
10, avenue d'Iéna
75016 Paris   Tel. 40.73.34.60

Librairie Dunod
Université Paris-Dauphine
Place du Maréchal-de-Lattre-de-Tassigny
75016 Paris   Tel. 44.05.40.13

Librairie Lavoisier
11, rue Lavoisier
75008 Paris   Tel. 42.65.39.95

Librairie des Sciences Politiques
30, rue Saint-Guillaume
75007 Paris   Tel. 45.48.36.02

P.U.F.
49, boulevard Saint-Michel
75005 Paris   Tel. 43.25.83.40

Librairie de l'Université
12a, rue Nazareth
13100 Aix-en-Provence   Tel. (16) 42.26.18.08

Documentation Française
165, rue Garibaldi
69003 Lyon   Tel. (16) 78.63.32.23

Librairie Decitre
29, place Bellecour
69002 Lyon   Tel. (16) 72.40.54.54

Librairie Sauramps
Le Triangle
34967 Montpellier Cedex 2   Tel. (16) 67.58.85.15
Tekefax: (16) 67.58.27.36

A la Sorbonne Actual
23, rue de l'Hôtel-des-Postes
06000 Nice   Tel. (16) 93.13.77.75
Telefax: (16) 93.80.75.69

GERMANY – ALLEMAGNE
OECD Publications and Information Centre
August-Bebel-Allee 6
D-53175 Bonn   Tel. (0228) 959.120
Telefax: (0228) 959.12.17

GREECE – GRÈCE
Librairie Kauffmann
Mavrokordatou 9
106 78 Athens   Tel. (01) 32.55.321
Telefax: (01) 32.30.320

HONG-KONG
Swindon Book Co. Ltd.
Astoria Bldg. 3F
34 Ashley Road, Tsimshatsui
Kowloon, Hong Kong   Tel. 2376.2062
Telefax: 2376.0685

HUNGARY – HONGRIE
Euro Info Service
Margitsziget, Európa Ház
1138 Budapest   Tel. (1) 111.62.16
Telefax: (1) 111.60.61

ICELAND – ISLANDE
Mál Mog Menning
Laugavegi 18, Pósthólf 392
121 Reykjavik   Tel. (1) 552.4240
Telefax: (1) 562.3523

INDIA – INDE
Oxford Book and Stationery Co.
Scindia House
New Delhi 110001   Tel. (11) 331.5896/5308
Telefax: (11) 332.5993
17 Park Street
Calcutta 700016   Tel. 240832

INDONESIA – INDONÉSIE
Pdii-Lipi
P.O. Box 4298
Jakarta 12042   Tel. (21) 573.34.67
Telefax: (21) 573.34.67

IRELAND – IRLANDE
Government Supplies Agency
Publications Section
4/5 Harcourt Road
Dublin 2   Tel. 661.31.11
Telefax: 475.27.60

ISRAEL – ISRAËL
Praedicta
5 Shatner Street
P.O. Box 34030
Jerusalem 91430   Tel. (2) 52.84.90/1/2
Telefax: (2) 52.84.93

R.O.Y. International
P.O. Box 13056
Tel Aviv 61130   Tel. (3) 546 1423
Telefax: (3) 546 1442

Palestinian Authority/Middle East:
INDEX Information Services
P.O.B. 19502
Jerusalem   Tel. (2) 27.12.19
Telefax: (2) 27.16.34

ITALY – ITALIE
Libreria Commissionaria Sansoni
Via Duca di Calabria 1/1
50125 Firenze   Tel. (055) 64.54.15
Telefax: (055) 64.12.57
Via Bartolini 29
20155 Milano   Tel. (02) 36.50.83

Editrice e Libreria Herder
Piazza Montecitorio 120
00186 Roma   Tel. 679.46.28
                                     Telefax: 678.47.51

Libreria Hoepli
Via Hoepli 5
20121 Milano   Tel. (02) 86.54.46
                                     Telefax: (02) 805.28.86

Libreria Scientifica
Dott. Lucio de Biasio 'Aeiou'
Via Coronelli, 6
20146 Milano   Tel. (02) 48.95.45.52
                                     Telefax: (02) 48.95.45.48

JAPAN – JAPON
OECD Publications and Information Centre
Landic Akasaka Building
2-3-4 Akasaka, Minato-ku
Tokyo 107   Tel. (81.3) 3586.2016
                                     Telefax: (81.3) 3584.7929

KOREA – CORÉE
Kyobo Book Centre Co. Ltd.
P.O. Box 1658, Kwang Hwa Moon
Seoul   Tel. 730.78.91
                                     Telefax: 735.00.30

MALAYSIA – MALAISIE
University of Malaya Bookshop
University of Malaya
P.O. Box 1127, Jalan Pantai Baru
59700 Kuala Lumpur
Malaysia   Tel. 756.5000/756.5425
                                     Telefax: 756.3246

MEXICO – MEXIQUE
OECD Publications and Information Centre
Edificio INFOTEC
Av. San Fernando no. 37
Col. Toriello Guerra
Tlalpan C.P. 14050
Mexico D.F.
                   Tel. (525) 606 00 11 Extension 100
                        Fax : (525) 606 13 07

Revistas y Periodicos Internacionales S.A. de C.V.
Florencia 57 - 1004
Mexico, D.F. 06600   Tel. 207.81.00
                                     Telefax: 208.39.79

NETHERLANDS – PAYS-BAS
SDU Uitgeverij Plantijnstraat
Externe Fondsen
Postbus 20014
2500 EA's-Gravenhage   Tel. (070) 37.89.880
Voor bestellingen: Telefax: (070) 34.75.778

NEW ZEALAND –
NOUVELLE-ZÉLANDE
GPLegislation Services
P.O. Box 12418
Thorndon, Wellington   Tel. (04) 496.5655
                                     Telefax: (04) 496.5698

NORWAY – NORVÈGE
NIC INFO A/S
Bertrand Narvesens vei 2
P.O. Box 6512 Etterstad
0606 Oslo 6   Tel. (022) 57.33.00
                                     Telefax: (022) 68.19.01

PAKISTAN
Mirza Book Agency
65 Shahrah Quaid-E-Azam
Lahore 54000   Tel. (42) 353.601
                                     Telefax: (42) 231.730

PHILIPPINE – PHILIPPINES
International Booksource Center Inc.
Rm 179/920 Cityland 10 Condo Tower 2
HV dela Costa Ext cor Valero St.
Makati Metro Manila   Tel. (632) 817 9676
                                 Telefax : (632) 817 1741

POLAND – POLOGNE
Ars Polona
00-950 Warszawa
Krakowskie Przedmieácie 7   Tel. (22) 264760
                                     Telefax : (22) 268673

PORTUGAL
Livraria Portugal
Rua do Carmo 70-74
Apart. 2681
1200 Lisboa   Tel. (01) 347.49.82/5
                                     Telefax: (01) 347.02.64

SINGAPORE – SINGAPOUR
Gower Asia Pacific Pte Ltd.
Golden Wheel Building
41, Kallang Pudding Road, No. 04-03
Singapore 1334   Tel. 741.5166
                                     Telefax: 742.9356

SPAIN – ESPAGNE
Mundi-Prensa Libros S.A.
Castelló 37, Apartado 1223
Madrid 28001   Tel. (91) 431.33.99
                                     Telefax: (91) 575.39.98

Mundi-Prensa Barcelona
Consell de Cent No. 391
08009 – Barcelona   Tel. (93) 488.34.92
                                     Telefax: (93) 487.76.59

Llibreria de la Generalitat
Palau Moja
Rambla dels Estudis, 118
08002 – Barcelona
                   (Subscripcions) Tel. (93) 318.80.12
                   (Publicacions) Tel. (93) 302.67.23
                                     Telefax: (93) 412.18.54

SRI LANKA
Centre for Policy Research
c/o Colombo Agencies Ltd.
No. 300-304, Galle Road
Colombo 3   Tel. (1) 574240, 573551-2
                               Telefax: (1) 575394, 510711

SWEDEN – SUÈDE
CE Fritzes AB
S-106 47 Stockholm   Tel. (08) 690.90.90
                                     Telefax: (08) 20.50.21

Subscription Agency/Agence d'abonnements :
Wennergren-Williams Info AB
P.O. Box 1305
171 25 Solna   Tel. (08) 705.97.50
                                     Telefax: (08) 27.00.71

SWITZERLAND – SUISSE
Maditec S.A. (Books and Periodicals - Livres
et périodiques)
Chemin des Palettes 4
Case postale 266
1020 Renens VD 1   Tel. (021) 635.08.65
                                     Telefax: (021) 635.07.80

Librairie Payot S.A.
4, place Pépinet
CP 3212
1002 Lausanne   Tel. (021) 320.25.11
                                     Telefax: (021) 320.25.14

Librairie Unilivres
6, rue de Candolle
1205 Genève   Tel. (022) 320.26.23
                                     Telefax: (022) 329.73.18

Subscription Agency/Agence d'abonnements :
Dynapresse Marketing S.A.
38 avenue Vibert
1227 Carouge   Tel. (022) 308.07.89
                                     Telefax: (022) 308.07.99

See also – Voir aussi :
OECD Publications and Information Centre
August-Bebel-Allee 6
D-53175 Bonn (Germany)   Tel. (0228) 959.120
                                     Telefax: (0228) 959.12.17

THAILAND – THAÏLANDE
Suksit Siam Co. Ltd.
113, 115 Fuang Nakhon Rd.
Opp. Wat Rajbopith
Bangkok 10200   Tel. (662) 225.9531/2
                                     Telefax: (662) 222.5188

TUNISIA – TUNISIE
Grande Librairie Spécialisée
Fendri Ali
Avenue Haffouz Imm El-Intilaka
Bloc B 1 Sfax 3000   Tel. (216-4) 296 855
                                     Telefax: (216-4) 298.270

TURKEY – TURQUIE
Kültür Yayinlari Is-Türk Ltd. Sti.
Atatürk Bulvari No. 191/Kat 13
Kavaklidere/Ankara
                         Tel. (312) 428.11.40 Ext. 2458
                                     Telefax: (312) 417 24 90
Dolmabahce Cad. No. 29
Besiktas/Istanbul   Tel. (212) 260 7188

UNITED KINGDOM – ROYAUME-UNI
HMSO
Gen. enquiries   Tel. (171) 873 8242
Postal orders only:
P.O. Box 276, London SW8 5DT
Personal Callers HMSO Bookshop
49 High Holborn, London WC1V 6HB
                                     Telefax: (171) 873 8416
Branches at: Belfast, Birmingham, Bristol,
Edinburgh, Manchester

UNITED STATES – ÉTATS-UNIS
OECD Publications and Information Center
2001 L Street N.W., Suite 650
Washington, D.C. 20036-4922   Tel. (202) 785.6323
                                     Telefax: (202) 785.0350

Subscriptions to OECD periodicals may also be placed
through main subscription agencies.

Les abonnements aux publications périodiques de
l'OCDE peuvent être souscrits auprès des principales
agences d'abonnement.

Orders and inquiries from countries where Distributors
have not yet been appointed should be sent to: OECD
Publications Service, 2, rue André-Pascal, 75775 Paris
Cedex 16, France.

Les commandes provenant de pays où l'OCDE n'a pas
encore désigné de distributeur peuvent être adressées à :
OCDE, Service des Publications, 2, rue André-Pascal,
75775 Paris Cedex 16, France.

1-1996

OECD PUBLICATIONS, 2, rue André-Pascal, 75775 PARIS CEDEX 16
PRINTED IN FRANCE
(91 96 01 1) ISBN 92-64-14690-3 – No. 48411 1996